Living with a
Rottweiler

Edited by Kate Pinches

BARRON'S

The Question of Gender
The "he" pronoun is used throughout this book in favor of
the rather impersonal "it," but no gender bias is intended.

Baker & Taylor 3-1-05 $14.95

ACKNOWLEDGMENTS

Many thanks to Theresa Stockman (Tattanhoe), Betty Sherring (Jetauric),
Pat Bryant (Tronasta), Paula Timbrell (Eskada), and Bev Kimber (Bevanray).

First edition for the United States and Canada published
2001 by Barron's Educational Series, Inc.

Copyright © 2000 Ringpress Books

All inquiries should be addressed to:

Barron's Educational Series, Inc.
250 Wireless Boulevard
Hauppauge, New York 11788
http://www.barronseduc.com

International Standard Book Number: 0-7641-5327-7

Library of Congress Catalog Card No: 00-105774

Printed in Singapore
9 8 7 6 5 4 3 2 1

CONTENTS

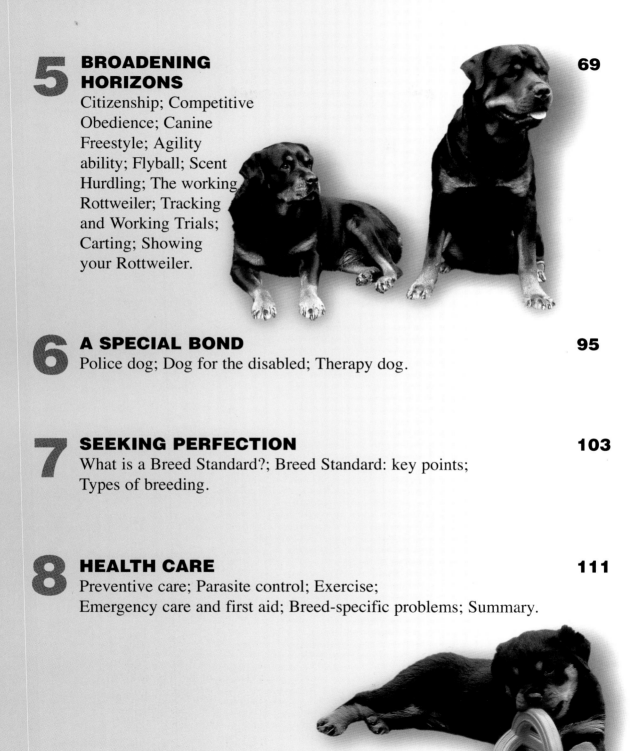

CHAPTER ONE

INTRODUCING THE ROTTWEILER

The Rottweiler breed is magnificent and oozes charisma. These are dogs with a powerful build, handsome good looks, an expressive face, and wonderfully hypnotic eyes. A good example of the breed is a joy to behold, whether he is standing proudly, intently surveying his surroundings, or trotting around a show ring, or racing around the backyard playing with a ball.

He doesn't simply look good, however. Personality-wise, the Rottie is a breed apart. His great intelligence, versatility, and incredible loyalty complete the package. With so many qualities, it is not difficult to see why he is such a popular choice with dog owners—not just in Germany, but all around the world, particularly in the United States and the United Kingdom.

ROMAN ROOTS

Although he is a relative newcomer to the canine world, first entering the U.S. in the late 1920s and the U.K. in the 1930s, the Rottie's roots seem to be ancient.

It is believed that the breed's progenitors were the Molosser dogs of the Romans. These were mastiff-type dogs that were used for fighting in coliseums and guarding emperors' palaces. Their most important function was as war dogs, however, accompanying the invading troops on their European conquests.

In the pre-refrigerator days of the first century A.D., the easiest way of ensuring that the troops were fed was to have a walking pantry! The cattle would be killed as needed. This not only eliminated storage and transportation difficulties—why carry a dead cow, when a living one has four perfectly good legs of its own?—but also ensured that the food was fresh. A good dog was, therefore, vital. He had to drive, and guard, the herd.

Around 74 A.D., the Romans had marched through the Alps, and had taken up occupation of the area of south Germany, close to the Alsace,

The breed takes its name from the German town of Rottweil.

Swiss, and Austrian borders, which is now known as Baden-Württemberg. One of the key towns in this area was Rottweil, so named, once the Romans had left around 260 A.D., because of the red tiles and bricks of the town's houses.

It is likely that some of the Roman dogs settled in Rottweil, where they bred with native dogs. Their mastiff-type droving heritage would have been a welcome asset to Rottweil dogs, as cattle became an important part of the town's economy.

CATTLE DOGS

Rottweil boasted lush pastures, ideal for grazing. Its geographical location made it a good commercial center too, and the town soon became a flourishing center for cattle trading. Drovers brought their animals over long distances to the Rottweil market, from Switzerland, France, and Hungary.

It is possible that Rottweil's native drovers caught the eyes of the foreign traders and that they took examples back with them. The breed then developed through breeding with native dogs. It is also possible that this scenario was reversed. Some dog historians have proposed that it is quite likely, given the similarity of some of the Swiss Mountain Dogs to the modern-day Rottweiler, that Swiss cattlemen introduced their own dogs to the area, or at least bred them to Rottweil's dogs.

Some believe the German Bullenbeisser (ancestor of the Boxer) was introduced to the breed. This theory is supported by the fact that a tiger-striped coat—characteristic of the Bullenbeisser—is mentioned in the first Rottweiler Breed Standard.

PROTECT AND GUARD

Whatever the breed's influences, it is clear that the early Rottweil dogs were bred to drive cattle, sometimes over long distances, to guard their herds, and also to protect their owners.

The forest areas surrounding Rottweil were good hunting grounds for bears and boars. A dog was needed that could protect the herds against such voracious predators.

It seems the dogs were also taken out on hunting expeditions. Paintings in the area show dogs of similar appearance to the Rottweiler accompanying their owners on such hunts.

The powerful Rottweiler was used to guard cattle, and to protect both herd and herdsman.

HERDERS

Cattle dogs needed to be sturdy, not only to deal with bears, but also to deal with the cows, which were semiwild and far removed from the placid domestic cattle we are used to today.

A successful herder needed a good "eye" to stare the cattle into submission. A robust but agile physique was necessary, as was a strong jaw to nip the hocks of stubborn movers. These early dogs were smaller than the modern-day Rottie. Heavy dogs would have lacked the stamina for driving cattle for hundreds of miles, and would have been slow and clumsy when moving the herd. Tall dogs would also be likely to nip higher than the hock, possibly spoiling expensive cuts of meat.

SAFE BANKING

There are tales of the herdsmen selling their cattle at market and then celebrating in the local taverns. To ensure that their money was not stolen while they patronized Rottweil's hostelries, they tied it around the necks of their dogs—and they knew it would not be taken!

On the way home, too, the dogs were often entrusted with the cash—thieves were unlikely to mug a large, snarling dog, however desperate they were. Of course, the dog would also protect his owner to the last.

THE BUTCHER'S DOG

The Rottweiler was originally called the Rottweil Butcher's Dog. This is because he would herd the butcher's cattle from the market to the abattoir, and then pull the carcasses back on a cart.

Another use of the Rottweiler of that day was for bullbaiting. This cruel blood sport provided entertainment and betting opportunities for onlookers. It was also a means of violently exercising a bull before it was slaughtered, since it was believed by some that meat was more tender if an animal had been subjected to strenuous exercise immediately before it was killed. Bullbaiting was made illegal at about the same time that bearbaiting was outlawed, although other canine blood sport events continued for many more years.

DECLINE AND FALL

The growth of the rail system toward the end of the 19th century saw the demise of the Rottweil

The Rottweiler's ability to guard and to protect made him an ideal police dog.

cattle dog. The government, which ran the rail network, forbade the herding of cattle in favor of train transportation. The Rottweiler continued to pull carts carrying milk and other goods for a while, but then even his role as a draft dog became defunct. Although several dogs were scattered elsewhere in Germany and neighboring countries, by 1905 there was said to be just one Rottweiler female in the breed's hometown.

LAW ENFORCEMENT

The breed was saved from possible extinction by its talents as a working dog. The Rottweiler caught the attention of the German police at the start of the 1900s. Rumor has it that an off-duty policeman, out walking his pet Rottweiler, encountered some brawling drunks. He managed to deal with the mini-riot quickly and efficiently thanks to his brave dog.

The first two Rottweiler police dogs—Max von der Strahlenburg and Flock von Hamburg—excelled in their duties, and it became clear that the breed's fortitude, intelligence, and natural instincts to guard and protect proved these dogs to be ideal candidates. In 1910, the Rottweiler was officially accepted as the fourth police dog breed (the others were the German Shepherd, the Airedale Terrier, and the Doberman Pinscher).

The Rottie was so suited to his new occupation that police organizations initiated their own breeding programs, and so the Rottweiler's numbers grew.

The breed's popularity outside the police force also increased. As a police dog, the Rottweiler was seen by many members of the public, who admired the breed's talents and who started to take them into their homes.

EARLY BREED CLUBS

The breed's association with the police extended beyond a working relationship. One club, the German Rottweiler Club (Deutscher Rottweiler Klub, DRK) was affiliated to the German Police Dog Association. First established in 1907, it produced many police dogs, and the club focused on maintaining the breed's working ability.

A second club, the South German Rottweiler Club, was incorporated into the International

A Breed Standard was drawn up detailing color, size, and conformation.

Rottweiler Club when it was formed shortly afterwards, also in 1907. This international club concentrated more on the Rottweiler as a show dog (although it was chaired between 1912 and 1915 by the police commissioner of Frankfurt).

Fortunately, the two clubs merged in 1921 to form a universal German Rottweiler club, the Allgemeiner Deutscher Rottweiler Klub, ADRK. The amalgamation was in the best interests of the breed, preventing the working/show split that has damaged so many other breeds. This commitment continued, with the club prohibiting the showing and breeding of any dogs that had not passed their working test.

DEVELOPING STANDARDS

As with all breeds of dog, the Rottweiler has developed over time. Even in the last 100 years there have been significant changes to the breed.

The first Breed Standard (the description of the ideal Rottie), written by Albert Kull from the International Club for Rottweilers and Leonbergers, appeared in 1883. It stated that the ideal height for a dog was 23.5 inches (60 cm), and the optimum weight was 66 pounds (29 kg)—two inches smaller and over half the weight of today's Rotties! It also allowed more color variations (including red) and endorsed a thick, reasonably long, abundant coat.

There were subsequent Standards, but the most significant was the one in 1921 by the ADRK, which finally declared that the only acceptable color was black with clear, defined mahogany to yellow markings. Before this time, color was of little importance—working ability was the only consideration.

In the 1926 ADRK publication, *Word and Picture*, it appears that two sizes of Rotties were permitted—the large draft dog, and the slighter-built cattle dog. With the ADRK's efforts to combine good looks and working ability, the two size distinctions became less apparent over time.

TO AMERICA

The Rottweiler reached America in 1929, when three Germans (Otto Denny, Fred Kolb, and August Knecht) emigrated to New York with their dogs.

The Rottie is one of the most popular breeds in North America.

August Knecht's Stina vom Felsenmeer was the first Rottie registered in the American Kennel Club Stud Book, in 1931. Stina had a litter the same year, which was the first AKC-registered litter of Rotts. Technically, Otto Denny had the first American Rottweiler litter, in 1930, but he recorded it in the German Stud Book rather than in the American one.

It was enthusiast Noel Jones who had the honor of handling the first three AKC Champions—the very first being Champion Zero in 1948. Noel was also responsible for establishing the Rottweiler Club of America, and held shows in his own backyard!

As elsewhere around the world, the Rottweiler gradually became increasingly popular. In 1940, there were just 11 Rotties registered with the AKC. Twenty years later, there were 77. Another 20 years later, in 1980, there were 4,701. From then on, there was a Rottie explosion, with registrations exceeding 100,000 in 1994. Although the figures have not quite reached such giddy heights since, the Rottie has remained one of the most popular breeds in North America.

TO GREAT BRITAIN

Thelma Gray was the first to introduce the Rottie to the U.K., in 1936. She imported three females (Enne vom Pfalzgau, Astra von Norden, and Diana von Amalienberg) and one male (Rozavel Arnolf von der Euchinger Ruine) from Germany, as foundation stock. During World War II, Thelma sent the dogs to Ireland for their safety, but was unable to trace them once peace had been declared. Sadly, the remaining Rottie

A big softie at heart, the Rottweiler needs an experienced, confident owner to bring out the best in him.

stock elsewhere in the U.K. was too old to be bred, and the breed died out.

The second phase of the British Rottie started in 1953 when Frederick Roy-Smith, a veterinarian with the Army Dog School in Germany, brought a male (Ajax von Führenkamp) and a female (Berny von Weyler) back with him to England. The female was not of the highest of standards, and neither was the singleton pup she produced, so Captain Roy-Smith brought another female to the U.K.— Rintelna Lotte von Oesterberg. Further dogs were imported, and the breed's popularity grew; however, it was nearly 20 years after Thelma Gray first introduced the Rottie that the Kennel Club recognized it as a breed and Challenge Certificates were offered in the show ring.

The breed has gone from strength to strength since then, with the Rottweiler becoming one of the most popular breeds of pedigree dog.

THE RIGHT OWNER

During the last 20 years, the Rottweiler has gained an unwarranted reputation for being an aggressive dog, and some people have latched onto the Rottie in order to feed a macho image. The noble Rottweiler, which can be a big softie at heart, doesn't deserve such an owner. Rather, he requires someone who is confident, firm, and gentle, and who appreciates his dogs, giving them the training, exercise, love, and respect they are entitled to. If this is you, read on!

CHAPTER TWO

PUPPY POWER

If you are reading this book, then you are probably pretty certain that you want a Rottie. But please think carefully whether this really is the right breed for you. Don't just choose a Rott because you like the look of the breed—beauty is only skin deep. For the sake of yourself, and the dog, consider the following.

- Cute little puppies grow into big, strong dogs. Do you have the space (in your home, yard, and car) to accommodate a Rottie?
- Big dogs are more expensive to maintain—they eat more, and veterinary bills are higher.
- A large dog needs considerable regular exercise—and won't be content with a daily five-minute jog up the street and back again.
- Do you have the time and commitment for continued training throughout the dog's life? Rotties are wonderful dogs, provided they are well trained and socialized.

- Can you commit to a dog for the next 14 years or so?
- Do you have the right personality to be a Rottie owner? Meek, timid owners need not apply! The Rottie needs someone he can respect, who has an air of authority. If you do not have the strength of character necessary, consider another breed.

Still reading? If you are absolutely sure that the Rottie is the only dog for you, devote your time to researching the breed thoroughly. Talk to as many owners and breeders as you can. Ask about the disadvantages of the breed as well as the advantages. Attend shows, read books, surf the Net. Once you have saturated yourself in Rottie facts, you will be in a better position to make an informed decision.

FINDING A GOOD BREEDER

The next job is to find a good breeder. This is important when dealing with any breed, but

Rottie puppies are irresistible—but remember, this is a large and powerful breed that requires a knowledgeable owner.

with the Rottie it is essential. The Rottweiler is a big, powerful dog. If you get one that does not have a 100 percent trustworthy temperament, you are asking for trouble. Your breed club or kennel club will be able to put you in contact with reputable breeders. Ask around for personal recommendations.

When you have found a good breeder with a litter, research the puppies' parentage. Socialization is important (page 31), but the foundations must be there first. If the dog's parents, grandparents, or great-great-grandparents have shown even a hint of aggression, steer clear. Rotties are not a rare breed, and you can choose to be fussy.

As well as researching the character of the line, the health should also be impeccable. Ask for details of any hereditary problems in the breed. Don't just take the breeder's word for it; ask to see the relevant documentation (hip certificates, etc.; see page 126).

A genuine breeder will believe that his or her responsibility for the pup does not simply come to an end when you hand over the cash. He or she will want to be kept informed about how

you are getting on, and will expect you to contact him or her for advice if you encounter any problems. He or she should also offer to take the puppy (or adult dog) back if you have any problems, or if your circumstances change.

Home Raising

Although many breeders raise puppies quite adequately in kennels, ideally they should be raised in the home. It is a lot more work for the breeder but is in the puppies' best interests. In a busy home environment, the puppies will grow up accustomed to all the sights, sounds, and smells of everyday life. Washing machines and

The puppies should be happy and healthy, showing an active interest in everything that is going on.

dishwashers will hold no fear for them and they will be used to children racing around and visitors coming and going. Consequently, your puppy will be more confident when facing the new experiences you will socialize him to when you get him home.

It goes without saying that the litter and premises should be clean. The puppies should appear happy, healthy, friendly, and playful.

- A Rottie pup has been compared to a little bear. He should be quite sturdy-looking and should have a plump, rounded body. A potbelly may indicate a heavy worm load.
- His eyes should be clear, bright, and full of life.
- His nose should be cold and wet.
- There should be no discharge from his eyes or nose.
- His bottom should be clean.
- His coat should be thick and clean, and there should be no evidence of fleas or flea dirt (little black specks).

The Ideal Pup

View the litter as early as the breeder will allow. Because of the risk of infection, you may be forbidden to touch very young puppies. Visit the litter regularly before you make your choice. Beware of the shy puppy that is nervous and reticent. He could develop into a fear-biter, and will need an experienced owner to instill confidence into him.

A fearless, bold puppy could also be inappropriate, by growing up to be too dominant for you. As a novice, the best puppy

The breeder will help you to assess temperament so you can choose the most suitable puppy for your lifestyle.

for you would be one that is confident but is not too bold. The breeder will know the puppies' personalities, and will be able to help you match your experience to the right one.

Character Test

There are numerous detailed temperament tests devised by behaviorists that help to assess a puppy's natural character. A simple one is to roll him gently onto his back with your hand when he is about six weeks old. Count to 30. If he struggles fiercely, biting and thrashing around for the entire count, it is likely that he has a strong dominant streak that could be difficult for the novice owner to handle, particularly when he grows up. The ideal response is for the puppy initially to struggle slightly, and then to settle down when he realizes you are dominant. A puppy that offers no resistance, and that does his best to avoid eye contact with you, is unresponsive to people, and will be as difficult to handle as the extremely dominant dog.

Test for dominance by rolling the puppy on his back, and seeing how much he struggles during a 30-second period.

It takes years of experience to judge whether a puppy is likely to be successful in the show ring.

Show Quality

If you want a puppy with show potential, ask the advice of the breeder. It is difficult for the inexperienced eye to spot a possible talent (and it isn't much easier for the experienced one). You should not simply assess the qualities of the puppy you have before you, but also anticipate how the puppy will grow and whether he will carry these qualities with him into adulthood (without developing faults along the way!).

All in all, it takes years of experience, and lots of luck to spot a showstopper, so ask the breeder for his or her opinion.

Male or Female?

When they are small, there will be little difference between the males and females in the litter. The males may be slightly larger, and their heads and muzzles broader. If you are a first-time Rottie owner, you would do well to choose a female. They are generally smaller, less dominant, and easier to handle and train. If you have a dog already, a male-female combination usually works well (males tend to quarrel with males, and females with females), though you will have to make sure that one or both of the dogs are neutered (see page 49) to avoid any unwanted pregnancies.

PREPARING FOR THE PUPPY

Once you have picked the right puppy for you and have secured your choice by paying the breeder a deposit, you should start preparing for the new addition to the family.

Shopping List

- Although the breeder is likely to give you a few days' worth of **food** for the puppy, it is worth stocking up beforehand. Ask the breeder for details of what the puppy has been fed. It is important that you do not change the diet while the puppy is settling into his new home (see page 28).

- Along with a **feeding bowl**, you should buy a **water bowl**. There are lots to choose from—ceramic, stainless steel, plastic, etc. Stainless steel bowls are a good first choice for a puppy, as they cannot be smashed or chewed.

- A **crate** is a necessity. These "cages" offer a safe place to put the puppy when you are unable to supervise him. They should be used wisely—at night, in the car, and for short periods during the day. A crate should

A crate is an invaluable investment, and your puppy will soon learn to regard it as his own special den.

never become a sin bin—a puppy prison where he is punished for being naughty. Filled with cozy bedding, toys, and chews, your puppy will soon learn to love his den.

- **Insurance**. Many puppies come with a few weeks' veterinary insurance from the breeder. If you are interested in continuing with the policy, ask the breeder for details. Dogs can get themselves into all sorts of scrapes—particularly puppies—and veterinary care can be costly. Having insurance will mean you will never have to worry about huge, unexpected bills.

- **Grooming set**. To keep your puppy looking in tiptop condition, you should buy a bristle brush, a metal comb, guillotine-type nail clippers, and a mild canine shampoo (see page 29).

- Puppies need to play, and if you don't provide them with something to chase, chew, and pounce on, they will devise their own games (with the cat, your slippers, etc.). Pet shops have a wide variety of **toys**. Don't just choose the cheapest or the cutest; consider your pup's safety. Rotties have strong jaws and can inflict considerable damage on most puppy playthings. Not only is this costly, but it can also be dangerous. Chewed-off fragments of small balls could be swallowed, causing choking or even death. Buy only the sturdiest toys. Squeakies are fun, but in order to make them malleable, the plastic is too soft to withstand a Rottie's jaws. Check toys regularly and replace them at the first hint of damage.

- **Puppy collar, leash, and tag**. Your pup will not be too happy wearing these at first, so make sure they are light and that the collar is soft, so he hardly notices he is wearing them. Get a small identification tag engraved with your details (many pet shops offer this service).

Puppy-proofing

Although your puppy will be a little bewildered when you first get him home, this won't last long, and he will soon be running, jumping, climbing, and generally causing chaos wherever he tumbles. Plants will be knocked over or chewed, tablecloths will be tugged (bringing down everything on the table), tassels on cushions, sofas, or rugs will be pulled out, and slippers may be urinated on. You name it, your pup can destroy it!

Before you get your Rottie pup home, hide everything away until he is older (much older!). China, vases, ornaments, etc. should all be safely stored, as should shoes, slippers, umbrellas, and handbags. Plants should also be put well out of reach (and never underestimate a puppy's reach), as many can be dangerous to dogs (ask your veterinarian/garden center for details).

Electrical wires are a particular hazard, and should be tucked away. Also pay attention to telephone cords and wires, which are equally tantalizing for curious puppies hell-bent on destruction!

Your backyard should also be made safe, securely fenced all around, with deep foundations to ensure that your Rottie can't dig his way out.

Make sure that your backyard is safe before you bring your puppy home.

Remember that your little puppy will grow quickly, so don't waste your time with small half-fences that will have to replaced within a matter of months. Be warned: Although they are heavy dogs, Rotties are excellent climbers—and can scale a tree (or fence) almost as well as a squirrel! Anything less than a 6-foot (1.83-m) fence is a cinch for a determined adult Rottie.

THE HOMECOMING

Plan to collect your Rottie in the morning. This will allow plenty of time to get him home and settled in before he is put to bed. If he has spent some happy, comforting hours with his new family, he will be a little more secure and contented when he faces his first night alone (see page 21). If you have children, it is advisable to choose a school day, so the puppy can settle in for a few hours before meeting the kids.

Arrange for someone to drive you to the breeder, so you can devote your attention (and your lap) to the puppy on the way home. This is far kinder than sticking him in a crate in the back of the car. He will, eventually, have to get used to traveling in a crate, but for his first, and possibly long, trip away from his canine and human family for the first time, it will get your relationship off to a good start if you can cuddle and reassure him.

Take along a soft towel to sit the puppy on, and to clean up any accidents. If it is a long trip, water and a bowl should also be taken. Ask the

breeder not to feed him immediately before the trip home, and perhaps ask him to give the puppy half a travel sickness pill. If a puppy is carsick once, he is likely to become sick again, so his first long trip should be as enjoyable as possible (see page 33).

Take your puppy out to the backyard as soon as you get him home. Let him stretch his legs, sniff around, and perhaps play (though he will probably be too busy investigating). He is also likely to need to relieve himself (see page 22). If you have an adult dog at home, it may be worth letting him into the yard to meet the new arrival at this time (see page 23).

FIRST-NIGHT NERVES

After a long, exciting day, full of new experiences, your puppy should be exhausted and desperately in need of a good night's sleep. You, too, will be exhausted, but your tiredness is likely to get worse before it gets better! Although your Rottie will need to sleep, he will be distressed at being alone for the first time, and will probably howl all night to call his mom and littermates to him.

Puppies have mastered the art of the heart-breaking cry—able to reduce the most hardened of owners to tears. Be strong and resist returning to him, however tempting it is. If you give in, your clever puppy will learn that bark equals owner, and owner equals love, comfort, and snuggling up in said owner's big warm bed. He has to learn to sleep alone at some point, so why not from the very start? He'll learn the

Give your puppy a chance to explore his new home.

rules in just a couple of nights, and you will have saved yourself from making a problem for yourself for the future.

Before settling him in his crate for the night, take him outside to relieve himself. Put him in his crate with some bedding, toys, and a chew in one end of the crate, and some newspaper at the other end. Don't make a big fuss over him when you say good-bye; just say *"Goodnight"* and go.

Puppies do not like to soil their sleeping area, so it is essential that a newspapered area is provided in the crate or pen for him to eliminate. This will help to reinforce his house-training, teaching him that he should take himself off to a designated area to eliminate.

First thing in the morning, let him out to relieve himself (then put some cucumber on the bags under your eyes!).

HOUSE-TRAINING

Breeders who rear in the home are only too happy to teach the puppies to eliminate outside, so by the time you bring your Rottie home, he should already be well on the way to being clean inside the house.

Puppies hate to dirty their sleeping areas and so naturally relieve themselves away from their beds. It's your job to teach him to go outside to do his business. Puppies are quite predictable creatures when it comes to toileting, and need to go at the following times:

- As soon as they wake
- Just before going to bed
- After a meal
- After exercise

Your intelligent Rottweiler will soon understand the rules of house-training.

- After periods of excitement (play, meeting someone new, etc.)
- Whenever you see him sniffing the ground or squatting

You should take your puppy out frequently throughout the day, at least every two hours initially. This reduces the chances of him having an accident, and gets him into good habits. The more he eliminates outdoors, the more he will go outside of his own accord when he feels the need to go. As he gets older, he can be taken out less frequently, until, eventually, he will ask you when he wants to go outside.

Regular Regime

Some owners run an outside tap, or trickle a pitcher of water on the ground to encourage the pup to urinate outside, but there is usually no need to resort to such measures. Just follow the following simple steps and you should have a clean pup in no time.

- Choose a spot in the yard that will become his regular toilet area. A paved area is a good choice because it is easy to clean, and you'll save yourself from having bleached patches on your prized lawn.

- Take the puppy to the area regularly, and be patient.
- If he relieves himself, say *"Busy,"* praise him, and reward him by playing in the yard before returning indoors.
- If, after five minutes, he doesn't perform, take him indoors. Keep a watchful eye on him and try again 15 minutes later.
- Introduce him to different surfaces—grass, concrete, gravel, etc.—there's nothing worse than being in the middle of nowhere on a country walk with a dog that is

about to burst because he will go only on tarmac!

There are always puppies that are a little slow to learn, but sticking to the toileting routine should produce the desired result eventually.

MEETING THE FAMILY
Resident Dog

Let your older dog and puppy meet each other in your backyard (your resident dog is likely to be less territorial about the yard than he is about your house). Allow them to investigate each other and make sure there are no bones, chews, or toys around that they could fight over. Your puppy will probably be submissive to the older

Supervise introductions, and then allow the resident dog and the puppy to establish their own pecking order.

dog, and, if he isn't, he will soon be persuaded to be. If your older dog is naturally submissive, he may be more than happy to be dominated by a bossy Rottie.

Leave them to arrange their own pecking order and support their decision by feeding the top dog first, petting him first, etc. The underdog will be quite happy with this arrangement, provided he keeps being reminded of his lowly position. Disagreements generally come about only if you have two very dominant dogs, or if you give them mixed signals about who is subordinate to whom.

If you supervise initial encounters, a Rottie and a cat will learn to live in harmony.

Feline Friends

Rottie puppies can be boisterous little creatures and your cat is unlikely to welcome the new addition with open arms. However, cats are survivors and will soon adapt to the puppy as long as you handle the introductions carefully, making sure he learns to treat the cat with respect.

- Both will be curious to meet the other, although tensions may run high. Act as calmly as possible or they will pick up on the nervous atmosphere.
- Introduce them in a room where the cat can jump up to somewhere safely out of the puppy's reach if she feels threatened.
- Put the puppy in his crate and let the cat investigate him safely while he is behind bars. If the cat is apprehensive, repeat the crate introductions until she is more confident. If she doesn't seem too freaked, let the puppy out, while you pet and reassure her.
- If the puppy gets too boisterous, tell him "*No*" firmly. Your puppy must realize that the

cat is an important part of the family, not a new toy to be leaped on.
- Some felines are scaredy-cats that simply run away from anything intimidating. This is the most difficult scenario, as your pup may be tempted to chase her if she runs away—great fun for an eight-week-old. If you do not stop your Rottie, this behavior will become habitual and pup and puss will forever be enemies.
- Don't have too high expectations. Yes, some cats and Rotties become firm friends, but not all do. Even if the cat dislikes the puppy, she should eventually get used to him and they will learn to respect each other's space.
- Do not leave them unsupervised until you are absolutely sure they are safe around each other.

CHILD'S PLAY

Rottweilers make great family pets provided they are well socialized with children from a young age and are taught to respect them. In most households, one person is usually more involved in looking after the family dog than the others are—feeding, walking, and training him. Because of this, the dog develops a closer bond with that person. This can cause problems when dealing with a dog that has strong guarding instincts, such as a Rottweiler, as he may be prone to protect this person and may even see himself as second-in-command, above the rest of the family.

It is important that everyone in the family, however small, is involved in the puppy's life—training, exercising, feeding, playing, and handling him. The following exercises should be done with the whole family, and will help to protect your Rottie against possible problem behaviors in the future.

Children and puppies must learn to respect each other.

PUPPY PLAY
Have a Ball

As we have seen, dogs view the world very differently from us, reading meaning into things we would consider inconsequential. Mostly, they view actions according to pack status. For example, if you have a fun game of ball with your puppy, you may tire of the play, or be called away, tossing a final ball for your Rottie before returning indoors. End of story. However, he may interpret your actions quite differently, believing he has "won" the trophy, and that you have stopped challenging him for it because he is of higher status.

It may sound paranoid to read so much into an innocent game, but when you are dealing with a dominant breed of dog, especially when children are around, you shouldn't take any chances, and must assert your authority in the language dogs understand.

Encourage your Rottie pup to retrieve balls and give them to you.

- Throw a ball for your puppy, and call him to you as soon as he picks it up.
- Say *"Give"* as you tug it gently, encouraging him to give it up. Or, bribe him with food. Most puppies will drop the ball instantly when you say *"Give"* and show them a treat. Eventually, through word association, he will drop the ball as soon as you command; and you can withdraw the treats.
- As soon as the puppy lets go of the ball, throw it for him to fetch again. This way, he is instantly rewarded for giving the ball back.

- At the end of every game, you should make sure that your pup brings you the ball. It may seem petty, but it will reinforce to him that you are pack leader.

Mouthing Off

It is natural for puppies to mouth their owner's hands, clothes, etc., but how you deal with the behavior will determine how gentle he is in the future. If you tolerate his biting, it may well continue into adulthood—which is totally unacceptable. From the first day that you bring your little Rott home, he should be taught to inhibit his bite. Good bite inhibition is crucial. Biting is the main reason why dogs are put to sleep in the first year of their lives. To save your puppy's life, and to prevent him biting someone when overexcited, make sure everyone sticks to the following rules.

- If your puppy mouths you, do not wag your finger at him, or wave your arms about. He will think it is part of the fun game.
- The moment your puppy mouths you, say "*No*" sharply, stand up, cross your arms, and ignore him. Do not even look at him. Puppies hate to be ignored, especially Rottie pups for whom owner approval is so important. Being ostracized from the pack, even temporarily, will make him think twice about how careful he is with his teeth in the future.
- Ignore the puppy even if he doesn't make contact with your skin. Sweaters, pant legs, etc., should all be out of bounds to the puppy.
- Along with the whole family being taught to respond correctly, visitors should also be

told what to do if mouthed. Your Rottie must learn that it is never acceptable to bite.

Eating Habits

Food is treasured by dogs. Their instincts come to the fore, instincts from when they lived in the wild and food meant survival. Some dogs feel threatened when they are interrupted while eating, and can develop into food guarders, snapping at anyone or anything that comes within lunging distance of the food bowl. Given their guarding qualities, this instinct is particularly strong in Rotties. It is your job to show that, far from being a threat to his

If treats are dropped into his food bowl, the puppy will learn to welcome the intervention rather than see it as a threat.

WORK WITH CHILDREN AND ANIMALS

To maintain harmony in the home, and to help avoid accidents, keep the following points in mind:

- Never leave a child and a dog (of any breed) together unsupervised.

- If you are thinking of getting a Rottweiler, and you have younger children, get a female. The female Rottie tends to be less dominant, and is likely to tolerate the antics of young children to a greater degree than the male.

- If you already have a Rottie and you are expecting a baby, take care that you do not ignore the dog. Your Rottie should know that the new baby is more important than he is, but do not give him grounds for jealousy. Involve the dog with the new arrival, and before too long, your Rottie will view the new baby as another member of his human herd, loving and protecting him as he has the rest of you.

- Do not let your children and your Rottie share a bed. Apart from encouraging your dog to think that he is more important than he is, you are increasing the chances of him developing a separation anxiety. If he becomes too close to your children, when they grow up and are out more, he will become very distressed by their absence.

- Make sure your children respect the dog. Boisterous games or teasing behavior may start off as fun, but, if things get out of hand, your children will get the worst of it. Even the gentlest creature can respond with a bite if pushed too far.

- Your children's friends should also be taught how to behave around your Rottie. Rough-and-tumble games are strictly forbidden—if your loyal Rott sees "his" child being attacked, he may not realize it is a game and may dive in to defend him.

---

food, people should be welcomed because, as pack leaders, they bring food and allow their subordinates (i.e., the dog) to share it.

- When you first get your puppy home, he will probably be on four meals a day. Each mealtime, put an empty bowl on the floor.

- He'll probably think you are crazy, and will want you to pick it up in order to put food in. Give him just a small amount, so that you will have to refill the bowl several times before he has had his full allocation. This way, you are teaching him that people bring food; they do not take it away.

- Practice this every mealtime, with different people (family and friends) feeding the pup.

Until now, people have put food in the bowl. How will your puppy react when his full bowl is taken away?

- Put a small amount of food in the puppy's bowl, and when he is in the middle of eating, take the bowl away, put in a small amount of fresh chicken (or something equally mouthwatering), then give it back to him. It won't take an intelligent Rottie long to work out that the interruption was more than worthwhile!

Again, a variety of people should do this exercise regularly, so that when your Rottie is fully grown, he will not take exception to being interrupted when eating.

CARE OF THE PUPPY
Feeding

At eight weeks old, your Rottie puppy will probably be on four small meals a day. Soon after getting him home, the number can be reduced to three. You will know when you should cut out one of the meals as your puppy will not be as interested in one of his meals. The quantity of food given at each meal will be increased as the number of daily meals decreases until, eventually, your Rottie will be fed just once or twice a day, according to your own preference.

You must follow the diet sheet provided by

To begin with, your puppy will need four meals a day.

the breeder. If, for any reason, you want to change what you feed your puppy, you should do so gradually to avoid any tummy upsets. Add a little of the new food to the puppy's meal. Gradually, over the course of several days, increase the new food, correspondingly decreasing the amount of the former food.

Exercise

Being a fast-growing, heavy breed, it is important that your puppy's body is given time to develop and is not put under any undue pressure until his skeleton is strong and fully formed. As well as limiting his exercise, you should make sure he does not climb the stairs, jump out of the car, or leap off the furniture, etc.

For the first couple of months, your Rottie will get all the exercise he needs through playing in the backyard. It will help if he is given short leash walking sessions in public places when he has had his puppy vaccinations, but these walks should be no more than five minutes long.

Around five months of age, leash walking can be increased to about 10 minutes, gradually increasing this amount as he gets older. Do make sure that you do not tire your Rottie by walking too quickly or too far.

When he is a year old, he can enjoy half an hour's leash walking, and by the time he is 15 months old, the sky is the limit—he can free-run to his heart's content.

When you exercise your puppy, do not see it as a chore; it is your special quality time together. Play games with him, talk to him, and have fun together.

A young puppy will get all the exercise he needs by playing in the backyard.

Grooming

Although the Rottweiler does not need much grooming, you should get your puppy used to being handled from a very young age. Grooming isn't simply about making your Rottie look smart; it improves your relationship with your dog. It also reinforces the fact that you are more important in the pack than your Rottie.

In the wild, dogs groom each other as an act of friendship. The pack leader, as the most important member of the group, has the right to decide who should groom him and when. Your Rottie needs to learn that he will accept being groomed whenever *you* decide to, not when he allows you to.

Put your puppy on the floor and stroke him. Gently brush him for just a few minutes. To get to the hard-to-reach spots (e.g., the belly), lie him on his side. Praise him for complying. If he struggles, gently restrain him with one hand (not difficult with an eight-week-old puppy), and continue grooming. Do not speak to him until he stops wrestling with you. As soon as he accepts your attention, praise him.

Just a few minutes a day will make grooming considerably easier. You will not be able to restrain an adult Rottie with one hand, but, if you regularly practice this grooming exercise, you won't have to.

Open Wide

Your Rottie should also get used to having his mouth checked by a variety of people. As before, if he is used to being handled thoroughly, and associates it with enjoyable experiences, it will make your life much easier when he is older.

- Put one hand over his muzzle and gently bring his top lip up with your fingers, exposing his top teeth. At the same time, gently pull his bottom lip down with the other hand. Say *"Teeth,"* praise him, and give him a treat.
- Progress to brushing his teeth and gums gently with a soft toothbrush with a tiny bit of doggie toothpaste on it. Always say *"Teeth"* so that he knows what to expect.

Pill Popping

There will be times when you will need to give your Rottie pills to swallow (regular worming treatments, etc.). Rottweilers are stubborn

A puppy must learn to be handled all over—and this includes allowing his mouth to be opened.

with one hand around the muzzle and jaws, and with the other hand, gently stroke his throat to encourage him to swallow.

• If he won't swallow, a pretend sneeze or blowing a puff of air on his face usually startles a pup into swallowing.

Pedicures

There's nothing worse than trying to trim the nails of an adult Rottie with ticklish feet. Avoid this by training your compliant puppy.

• When you are cuddling him and he is quite content and secure, gently touch his feet one by one, saying *"Feet."* Stop, and resume your cuddle. Repeat several times.

• Next, gently touch his pads, his toes, and between his nails. Again say *"Feet,"* and give him a treat for being so tolerant.

• When he needs his nails trimmed, say *"Feet,"* hold the foot securely with one hand, and shave off a small amount of nail using guillotine-type nail clippers. Always give a treat at the end.

Eventually, you may get to the stage where, when you say *"Feet"* and show him the clippers, your Rottie will lift up his feet of his own accord.

Terrible Teething

Young puppies chew, but the real challenge starts when they hit the teething phase, starting at around 16–28 weeks. This is when your puppy's 28 baby teeth will begin to be replaced by 42 adult ones. His gums will become red and swollen, and he will need to chew to relieve the pain. Chewing will also encourage the baby teeth

creatures, and trying to wrestle those strong jaws open while pushing a pill down is no mean feat. Even if you do manage this, it is quite likely he will pretend to swallow a few times, and will spit the pill out discreetly when you are not looking. Teach him to *want* to cooperate.

• Put your hand over the puppy's muzzle, lift his head back, open his mouth gently with your other hand, say *"Open,"* pop a treat in, and praise him.

• Once he's tasted what you've put in, he'll be less suspicious and more cooperative.

• Practice putting the treat far back on the tongue. Close the mouth, keeping it shut

Make sure your puppy has safe toys to chew, particularly when he is teething.

to shift, allowing the new teeth to emerge. The teeth are replaced in stages—from the incisors through to the molars—and the whole process can take several months.

Remember, chews must be durable. Nylon bones are particularly useful as they do not splinter into sharp, dangerous fragments that can be swallowed. Rawhide chewies are good treats when you must leave your puppy alone for a few hours. Rawhide toys made of pressed particles in untanned leather are best for small puppies, since the small pieces chewed from them can be swallowed without causing gastric distress.

HOUSEHOLD RULES

The Rottweiler is a dog that likes routine and needs to know his boundaries. It is important to set down the household rules from day one so the puppy knows where he stands. Every home is different and you may wish to add to (or ignore) some of the basic rules below:

- Jumping up should never be tolerated. When a puppy leaps up at you, he'll barely reach your knees; however, if he grows up thinking this bad habit is acceptable, as an adult he'll

be more than capable of flooring you! (See page 47.)
- The puppy should never be allowed on your bed, favorite chair, or sofa unless you give your permission. He should get off without a grumble whenever you ask.
- Begging should never be tolerated. As pack leader you should be able to eat undisturbed, feeding your Rottie his meal *after* you have finished yours.
- Your Rottie should be given attention when *you* allow it, not when *he* demands it. Nudging you for a cuddle when you are busy on a phone call is very endearing, but engenders bad habits.
- Your Rottie should sit and wait at the door (see page 46). This will stop him from barging into visitors, or racing out onto a busy street before you have control of him.

SOCIALIZATION

Socialization is the process of introducing your puppy to the world so that it holds no surprises or fears for him when he grows up. Familiarity is comfortable. We feel safe around people and places we know, and can feel unnerved if we are asked to do something new. The same is true of dogs. If you familiarize your puppy to a wide range of experiences, he will absorb them all like a dry sponge and will be more confident when he encounters them again when he is older.

Being a naturally suspicious breed, it is vital that the Rottie receive considerable socialization. If a dog feels threatened, he has

PUPPY SOCIALIZATION

Be inventive with your socialization—a puppy that encounters lots of new experiences will learn to be calm and confident.

two options: fight or flight. Most choose the former, believing that attack is the best form of self-defense. It is your job to make sure that your Rottie sails through life without being threatened, so get busy socializing!

Inside the Home

Up to 12 weeks of age, your puppy will be particularly sensitive to new situations and experiences. At this time, however, it is likely that he will be housebound, not yet being protected by his puppy vaccinations. It is, therefore, crucial that he receive as much socialization inside the home as possible, preparing him for when he is allowed safely to step out into the big, wide world.

Invite as many different people as you can to meet the puppy. They should all handle him and pet him. Visitors that bring treats will be particularly welcome.

Ask visitors to bring some props and have a socialization party in your backyard. Introduce your puppy to all the things he may see when walking down the street:

- Someone wearing a hat, sunglasses, and motorcycle helmet
- Someone carrying an umbrella
- Someone who can walk a baby carriage around your yard
- Someone who can rollerblade/cycle/skateboard past your puppy
- Someone playing with a yo-yo
- Someone talking on a cell phone
- Someone carrying balloons
- Someone playing a musical instrument (preparing him for holiday parades, etc.)

Sounds Around the Home

The home has many trouble spots too. Since this is where your Rottie will spend most of his time, he should feel utterly safe and secure there.

- Ask someone to drop a metal saucepan cover or bowl on the kitchen floor while you are in another room playing a fun game with the puppy. Do not react to the noise at all; just continue playing.
- The same response should be given when there are fireworks or thunder outside—do not reinforce his fear by cuddling him; you will simply be rewarding his nervous behavior.
- Vacuum cleaners can also terrify a little pup that has never seen a big noisy robot moving around the house before. Hopefully, your Rottie will have been introduced to a vacuum

cleaner at his breeder's house (the advantages of being home-reared).

- If he is still a little apprehensive, play a game with him.
- Ask someone to switch on the machine and leave it stationary in the corner. Because it doesn't move, he will get used to the sound, associating it with the fun he is enjoying from his game.
- By the time you progress to vacuuming in the same room as the puppy, he should be more confident. In fact, most puppies go the other way and end up play-attacking vacuum cleaners rather than running away from them.

Car Travel

Before he is allowed to go into public places, you can take your pup out in the car so that he can see the world from the comfort and safety of his crate.

- Put the crate in the back of the car, put a couple of toys in it, shut him in with them, and let him amuse himself for a few minutes. Give him a treat, take him out, and then have a game with a toy.
- After a few sessions of that, go for a short, gentle drive around the block, finishing with a treat and another game in the backyard.
- Gradually extend the length of the trips, incorporating busier areas, such as town centers, as your puppy gets more confident.

For the first few drives, your puppy may be prone to carsickness. As stated earlier, if he is sick once, he is likely to be sick again, so sit on the backseat of the car and watch him carefully while someone else drives. If you see him drooling, ask the driver to stop. Distract the puppy with a toy and only continue the short drive home when he is fully recovered.

Out and About

As soon as your Rottie is protected by his puppy vaccinations, you should take him out to as many places as possible.

- Walk him in a shopping center, taking advantage of any admirers that approach. The more he is fussed over by strangers (but only with your permission), the better.

When your puppy has completed his vaccination course you can go further afield and broaden his horizons.

- Walk around parking lots with him. This will get him used to slow-moving vehicles, preparing him for when you walk him along busier streets.
- Take a ride up and down an elevator.
- Walk your Rottie on a public footpath through a field of cows and sheep—but always make sure he is on a leash.

TRAINING

Rotties love training. Not only does it exercise their minds, but it also gives them an opportunity to serve, respect, and please you. All members of the family should be involved in the puppy's training, including children.

"Little and often" is the principle behind successful training. Five minutes five times a day is much better than a two-hour session once a week, when the puppy will become bored and rebellious and will forget everything he has learned by the next day. Short, fun sessions keep him (and you) fresh and wanting more.

Set time aside when you know you won't be interrupted. Ignore any ringing telephones or doorbells and concentrate on your dog. Always finish a session on a high note—when the puppy has done something right. Then reward him, and have a game together. Training should never become a chore; it is an important bonding opportunity between dog and handler, and should be fun, fun, fun! If you are tired or preoccupied, your sensitive Rottie will pick up on your negativity. Train only when you are able to give him your best. In all other instances, ask someone else in the house to train him.

The Rottweiler is a willing pupil, particularly when treats are being offered!

Reward-based Training

Would you work for nothing? Neither will your Rottie! To get the best out of him, you have to make it worth his while by rewarding him sufficiently with praise, treats, and games. Yes, it's a bribe, but it works, and it also makes the training process fun for your dog. And as long as he's enjoying himself, he is more likely to cooperate.

You should reward your Rottie every time he does something that you want him to. When he has got the hang of what is expected of him, you can start to give the rewards randomly. He will never know when he will get a treat, but he will still work hard for you just in case you have one.

Name Game

You should choose your puppy's name very soon after getting him home. Most breeders give their puppies names, but your puppy will be young enough to adapt to a name change if you decide his face doesn't fit the name he has been given.

To teach your Rottie his name, say it frequently whenever you talk to him. Make sure he associates it with good experiences—being cuddled, being praised, being fed, etc.

Recall

When the puppy knows his name, start teaching him to come when called.

- Sit a few feet from your pup, show him a favorite toy, and call *"Rover, come!"* Be very excited, and use a higher-pitched tone than your usual speaking voice. Clap your hands on your knees to hurry him to you.
- Give him a big hug and heaps of praise when he comes to you; act as if you are really very pleased to see him. Give him a treat as a "thank you" for being so obedient, and give him the toy to play with.
- Practice this exercise regularly, increasing the distance he has to come to you. Eventually, call him from one room to another, always praising and rewarding him for his trouble.

Outdoors, *recall* is more difficult as there are so many interesting things for the puppy to investigate. You will have to be more interesting than ever before; use the smelliest, tastiest treats possible (cooked liver is a favorite).

- Once your puppy has had his vaccinations, take him to a nearby park.
- Show him the treats you have in your pocket, give him one, put him on an extendible leash, and let him play/sniff, etc.
- After a few minutes, call your Rottie to you, and give him one of the treats. Immediately, send him back off to play.
- Throughout the walk, call him to you and reward each time.
- If he doesn't come, be more excited. Start throwing a ball up in the air and catching it (single-handed, as you are holding the leash with your other hand), start running away from him, make funny noises, etc.
- If he still doesn't come, you'll have to slowly bring him in by shortening the leash.
- Never shout at him if he refuses to come or when he does finally deign to share your company. If you are angry, it will only make him think twice about coming to you next time.

Get a good recall *going from an early age, making sure you always sound bright and excited so your puppy wants to come to you.*

Collar

When you are cuddling your puppy, put a soft, light collar on him, all the time petting and talking to him. He will probably not even realize it is on. If he does, throw him a ball to chase. If he is distracted, he won't try to scratch it off. Never leave the collar on while the puppy is unsupervized—accidents can happen, and if he catches the collar on something and can't get away, it could end in tragedy.

A tag with your name and telephone number can be attached to his collar, but you should also investigate more permanent forms of identification, such as microchipping. This is where a tiny microchip (the size of a grain of rice) is inserted between the dog's shoulder blades. When read with a scanner, it reveals a number that corresponds to your name and telephone number, so you can be traced if your dog is found.

Leash

For the first month or so, your Rottie will follow you around the house and will want to be beside you wherever you are. Exploit this! Put a light leash on his collar and encourage him to walk beside you. Keep the leash very loose so he doesn't feel that it is on. A tight leash will make him feel trapped and insecure, and he will try to pull away from it.

At around four months of age, puppies become more independent and are too busy investigating and amusing themselves to follow their owners around all day. At this stage, you will have to bribe your puppy to continue his leash training by luring him with a treat.

Work on your puppy's instinct to follow when you start leash training.

- Put him in the *sit* position (page 38) on your left side.
- Take a few steps forward, and when he walks beside you say *"Walk."* Stop and give him a treat.
- If he won't walk next to you, use the donkey and carrot routine—show him a treat and hold it just in front of him. As he walks forward to get it, walk forward with him, and say *"Walk."* After a few paces, praise him and give him the treat.
- Practice regularly, gradually refining his performance so he is right beside your knee, and close to you.
- The moment he pulls ahead, stop. Your Rottweiler is pulling because he wants to get somewhere (usually the park). He must learn that his actions are counterproductive; far from getting him there quicker, pulling means you stop, so he doesn't get there at all. Put him in the *sit,* and start again.
- If he lags behind, you need to motivate him. Walk a little quicker so he has to concentrate

on you to keep up, and, as soon as he achieves the right *heel* position, praise him and give him a treat. This should be sufficient motivation, sparking his interest again. Stop the training session as soon as he has achieved the right position so he doesn't become bored.

Don't give up on this exercise. You must teach your Rottie to walk beside you in an orderly, controlled manner. Every day, he will get older and stronger, and it will get harder to teach him (and to control him). It is much easier to teach him leash work while he is young, impressionable, and manageable.

By the time your puppy is ready to venture into the outside world, he should be walking confidently on the leash.

Sit

This exercise is very simple—after all, sitting isn't a foreign concept to a puppy; you just have to teach him to sit when you ask him to.

- When your puppy sits of his own accord, say *"Sit,"* praise him, and give him a treat. He'll be surprised at your reaction, but will welcome it nevertheless. This exercise is a useful way of teaching him what *"Sit"* means.

Next, teach him to sit when you ask him to.

- Show him a treat and hold it above his eyes.
- As he stretches his chin up to take the treat, move the treat back a little, so he has to stretch even further to get it.
- If he jumps up to get it, do not give it to him.
- After a few attempts he will realize that the only way he can get the necessary reach is to put his rear on the floor.
- As soon as he sits, say *"Sit,"* give him the treat, and tell him what a smart boy he is.
- Practice for a few minutes every day. Get him to sit before you give him his dinner, before going through doors, etc. It is good training revision, and also keeps his brain going.

Down

As with the *sit*, opportunist training—where you say *"Down"* whenever your puppy lies down—is useful for teaching the association between the word and the action.

- Put your puppy in the *sit* and show him that you have a treat in your hand.
- Put the treat in your closed fist, and put it on the floor.

Hold a treat above your puppy's head, and as he looks up, he will automatically go into the sit *position.*

- As with the *sit*, the puppy will try every which way to get to the treat, and will eventually realize that the best reach can be had by lying down.
- As soon as his belly touches the floor, say *"Down"* and give him the treat at once. Cuddle and praise him so he is left in no doubt that he has done something you approve of. The next time you hold the treat on the floor, it won't take your Rottie long to remember what he needs to do.

Lower a treat toward the floor, and your puppy will follow his nose, and go into the down.

Build up the stay exercise in early stages.

SAY AS HE DOES

If, when luring your pup with a treat, you tell him *"Sit,"* he will think that the word *"Sit"* means "Jump up and try to wrestle the treat out of my owner's hands," because this is what he has probably been doing! Only say the word *"Sit"* when he sits, so that he learns to associate the word with the action. This gives him no opportunity for error.

When he fully understands an exercise and will reliably *sit* or go *down* or *wait,* etc., when lured, then you can start using the command word so that, eventually, instead of you saying a command as he does the action, he will do the action as you say the command. In other words, the training rule "say as he does" soon leads to "do as I say," with the puppy obeying your commands.

Stay

This is one of the more challenging exercises, as it requires your ever-moving puppy to sit still! Again, you need to work out a handsome remuneration package—a payoff. To get the puppy to sit still, he needs to know that there will be plenty of fun and treats at the end of it.

- Put your Rottie in a *sit.*
- Take one step back, raise your hand at arm's length with the palm facing him, and say *"Stay"* firmly.
- Count to three, step forward, and praise and treat him.
- Gradually increase the distance and length of the *stay.*
- If he starts having difficulties, shorten the distance and the length of the *stay* to increase his confidence again.
- Practice throughout the day in different places so that he will eventually reliably *stay* wherever he is.

CHAPTER THREE

THE ADOLESCENT ROTTWEILER

Provided you have put in all the hard work in the first few months of a puppy's life, adolescence should not produce too many headaches or tears. However, this is not to underestimate the radical transformation that your tiny, manageable Rottie puppy can undergo, emerging from adolescence as a 112-pound (51-kg) hulking beast. If you never quite managed to get around to teaching him to walk well on the leash, you will really have your work cut out now—and will develop the biceps of Hercules in your vain attempts not to be dragged around the park behind him.

The sheer weight of a Rottie produces its own problems, especially during adolescence, when your Rottie's brain is that of a puppy, but his body is getting bigger every day. It's very important that your adolescent has been thoroughly trained and socialized and that he will respond to your instructions without fail (see Chapter Two).

PUBLIC DUTY

We all know the general public's terrible perception of the Rottweiler. The image of the evil Devil Dog, as seen in numerous Hollywood films, is firmly imprinted on the minds of many people, most of whom have never even met a Rottie. When you are in a public place, your Rottie is an ambassador for the breed. One growl, and onlookers will condemn every Rottweiler in the country.

Don't be surprised if people cross the street when you take your faithful companion for a walk. Although it is hurtful when someone judges your dog on looks alone, you shouldn't take it personally. With time, you will develop an immunity to such reactions, learning to take it all in your stride. As long as you love—and have pride in—your dog, that's all that counts.

Also, be prepared to have Rottie admirers approaching you all the time, thumping your dog on the head with a hearty pat, and telling

The Rottweiler is such an impressive dog, he is likely to attract attention wherever he goes.

you at length how they've always wanted one of these dogs because they are so "tough."

For a dog that is naturally wary of strangers, and is so attuned to the moods around him, both reactions can be unnerving. As before, socializing your puppy to as many people and situations as possible is vital. This cannot be stressed enough. If your dog fears nervous people or aggressive people or any kind of people, and reacts defensively (a natural reaction in any dog), he may not only seriously injure someone, but is likely to pay for his mistake with his life.

If you have a well-trained, loving, and lovable Rottie, it's not so much a case of protecting people from him, but of protecting him from other people. Always think ahead to any

possible problems you may encounter. For example, if you are exercising in a busy park where small dogs and children are present, don't let your Rottie off the leash.

It seems unfair to punish the dog for other people's prejudices, but it is better to be safe than sorry. The Rottweiler is a powerful breed, and can easily injure a tiny Yorkie, or a toddler, in boisterous, overenthusiastic play, so don't take any chances.

DOG–DOG AGGRESSION

Early puppy and socialization classes, with lots of positive interaction with all kinds of dogs, should ensure that your Rottie is friendly with other canines. Running free in a park, playing with doggie friends of similar size, your dog is likely to be happy and carefree, but put a leash on a Rottie and his mood can change.

When he is walking beside you in a public place, your dog's natural guarding instincts can take hold. You must be calm and confident at all times. Once attached, the leash becomes like a telephone hotline direct from you to your dog, passing on all your moods and anxieties.

Of course, it is easy to get into a Catch-22 situation. If your dog does growl at another dog, you will understandably be anxious the next time he encounters one. Your Rottie will detect your unease, and will naturally wish to protect you against the perceived threat—by growling to warn off the dog. And so the situation escalates in ever-increasing circles.

There are two ways of breaking the cycle— keeping watch and going back to basics.

Do not let your Rottie switch into "guard dog" mode.

Keeping Watch

Don't let your Rottie switch into "guard dog" mode. Anticipate possible problems and divert your dog's attention. If you see another dog approaching, put your Rottie in the *sit,* and tell him to *"Watch"* you. Keep treats in your pocket to be used as a reward for giving you his undivided attention.

Set aside five minutes several times a day to teach this command.

- Put your Rottie in the *sit,* and show him a treat. This should immediately get his attention!
- Lift the treat up to your face, and hold it level with your eyes. He will follow the treat with his eyes, and will end up looking straight at you.

- When your Rottie's eyes meet yours, say *"Watch,"* praise him, and reward him with the treat.
- Spend just two or three minutes, four or five times a day, on this exercise, until your Rottie understands what is expected of him.
- With time, he will learn to look at you, without you having to hold up the treat. Always reward him at the end of the session, though, so he doesn't lose interest.
- Practice holding his attention for gradually increasing periods, and repeat the command to maintain his attention.
- When he will reliably watch you in your home, practice in the backyard. Add distractions; ask someone in the family to walk past, for instance.
- Progress to increasingly busier places, such as the park, making sure you are calm and confident when you give the command.

Back to Basics

Along with managing your dog's on-leash hostility to other dogs by using the *watch* command, you should also try to solve the root cause of the problem. This means going back to basics—reminding your Rottie to behave with courtesy and good manners to his fellow dogs.

Seek the services of a local dog trainer, who will be able to advise you. Professional trainers often have bomb-proof dogs, whose help is enlisted in such cases. Having a calm, submissive dog walking past your Rottie at a distance—one that doesn't respond to your dog's growling and posturing—will give your

Work at getting your dog's attention with the watch command.

dog confidence that maybe he doesn't need to defend you after all. The moment a dog growls back, your Rottie will feel justified in his initial aggression, so a well-socialized "stooge" dog is essential.

Rehabilitation may be a prolonged process, but is well worth it for the peace of mind, the improvement in your dog's quality of life, and for the privilege of no longer having to wrestle your Rottie away from other dogs.

PEOPLE AGGRESSION

Aggression toward people is an altogether different scenario. This can be managed only by a professional animal behaviorist. Although dominance can sometimes be a cause of aggression in Rottweilers, *never* attempt to "teach the dog who's boss" by physically disciplining him. Aggression breeds aggression, and the situation will only get worse. The moment your Rottie shows any aggression, seek professional help immediately. Your veterinarian may be able to recommend a recognized professional. If not, your kennel club should be able to give you the details of behavioral organizations.

Leadership

The following simple exercises can help to earn your Rottie's respect, and prevent him from developing dominance aggression toward you. These exercises are not cures for dominance. As previously stated, you must *never* try to deal with such behavior on your own. Rather, these exercises are intended to prevent your relationship from deteriorating to a level where the dog feels he needs to be aggressive to you. These exercises will never be successful if they are not practiced within the framework of a stimulating, loving relationship with your dog.

Pack Position

Years of domestication have done little to dampen a dog's core instincts—impulses that have been present in wild dogs and wolves for tens of thousands of years. The most important thing in a dog's life is the pack, which enables all its members to survive—to hunt together, to raise pups, to ward off danger, etc. The pack's social structure is crucial for it to function properly.

The well-socialized Rottie will accept his subordinate status, and will understand that your word is law— even when it means making friends with the family rabbit!

The most important member of the pack, the pack leader, would be served by junior dogs. The leader would be entitled to eat first, discipline his subordinates, pick the best spot to sleep, etc. A weak leader would soon be ousted by a younger, stronger, ambitious member of the pack.

You are the pack leader, and your Rottie is your subordinate. This is not to say that you need to go around asserting yourself over the dog like some power-crazed tyrant. That is just cruel, and your dog will not respect you for it. In the wild, a pack leader rarely has to punish the lower-ranking members because they know the boundaries and dare not overstep them.

Sweet Dreams

Just as the pack leader is entitled to sleep in the best spot, so you should do the same! Of course, you can let your Rottie sleep on the bed every now and again—but only when you tell him that it is okay, and he must get off as soon as you instruct him to.

Starting when your Rottie is still young, you should get him used to your house rules and enforce them.

- Tell your dog *"Off"* every time you find him on the bed or the sofa, when he has crept on of his own volition.
- When he has been well behaved, reward him with a cuddle on the sofa. He must realize that you are allowing him to share one of your many privileges, but only because you choose to give it. And just as you can give it, so you can also take it away.
- After a short time on the sofa, tell him *"Off"* and point to the floor. When he does as he is told, praise him.

Food

The pack leader should also eat first, and should be allowed to eat undisturbed; that means no begging!

- Feed your Rottie after you have finished your breakfast and/or evening meal.
- Never feed him scraps directly from the table—it encourages very bad manners.

Your Rottie will soon learn to sit quietly while you eat, knowing he will be fed soon afterwards. Because he should respect you as the pack leader, he will respect your right to eat first (to get the best "pickings" of the caught prey) and will accept his lowly position.

However, if you have been in the least bit inconsistent, then he will forever beg. Hope springs eternal, as they say, and your Rottie will cling to the glimmer of hope that, eventually, you will give in to his begging.

Doors

Just as you would allow a social superior to go through a door ahead of you (you wouldn't barge past your boss on the way to the lunchroom, would you?), your Rottie should allow *you* to walk through first.

Again, this is one of the privileges conferred on a pack leader. This will be recognized by your Rottie as a sign of your higher status. Plus, it makes everyday life much easier—bringing in the groceries and negotiating the front door is tricky at the best of times; trying not to trip over a hefty dog under your feet makes it even more difficult.

Make sure you are always the first to walk through a doorway.

If you want your dog to walk ahead of you, there is no law to say he can't. But it should occur only when you tell him to do so, not because you cannot control him.

- Stand a couple of paces from a door.
- Tell your dog *"Sit"* and *"Wait"* (see Chapter Two).
- Walk through the door, wait a few seconds, and walk back to your dog, praising him profusely for doing as he was told.
- If he attempts to follow, tell him *"No"* firmly, and put him back in the *sit* and *wait* position.
- Keep persevering. Rotties are not stupid, and if your dog knows his efforts at racing ahead of you will be in vain, he'll soon learn to conserve his energy.

- When he will reliably *sit* and *wait* as you walk ahead, put him on the leash, and walk forward toward the door with the dog walking beside you (see Leash Walking, Chapter Two).
- Open the door, and tell him *"Walk on,"* and guide the leash so that he is encouraged to walk ahead of you. He must do this only when you have given your permission for him to walk in front.

JUMPING UP

All breeds of dog will jump up on their owners, friends, or family, unless taught to do otherwise. It's just the dog's way of trying to get close to his loved ones and get their undivided attention.

In most breeds, having a bouncy dog results in no more than pawprints on your sweater, and a few surface scratches on your arm. A Rottie, however, is a powerful dog, and at adolescence he won't know his own strength. When he is a full-fledged adult, he will have even more muscle and weight, and will be more than capable of knocking over the strongest of people, let alone children or the elderly.

If, despite early training, your Rottie can't keep four feet on the floor, try the following.

- Every time you, a family member, or anyone else the dog is fond of, comes in, put your Rottie in the *sit* and tell him *"Wait."*
- If he leaps up, he should be reminded to *sit.*
- If he doesn't, turn away from him, cross your arms, and ignore him. No one should react to him in any way. Even saying *"No"* and

The mighty Rottweiler can be a real menace if he jumps up.

shouting at him is giving the dog what he wants—attention.
- When your Rottie calms down and sits quietly, then he should be praised and petted.
- If this attention gets him overexcited again, and he leaps up, ignore him as before.

HOME GUARDING

If people unfamiliar to your Rottie enter your home, he may not be quite so friendly. During adolescence, particularly, a Rottie's hormones can encourage him to become territorial. As we have seen, the Rottie is born to guard. Although it is a deep instinct in the breed, guarding should never be encouraged.

Yes, it is useful to have a dog that barks when someone knocks on the front door, but that is as far as it should go. You should never end up in the situation where you can't allow nonfamily members in your home for fear of how the dog will react. There are always times when you need to interact with people—the mailman, deliveryman, window cleaner, etc.—and if your dog is territorial, it is a disaster waiting to happen.

Early socialization, where as many people as possible are invited to your home to meet the puppy, is crucial, but this socialization should continue throughout the dog's life. Give a quarter of a cookie to visitors—not to dunk in their tea, but to give to the dog! Ask them to

The Rottie has an inborn instinct to guard, but make sure this behavior remains within your control.

tell the dog to *"Sit,"* and to give the cookie to him once he has done so. Open bribery, I know, but it works!

If your Rottie becomes territorial and you have even the tiniest nagging doubt as to how far he can be trusted with visitors, consult a professional dog behaviorist immediately.

SEPARATION ANXIETY

The Rottweiler forms strong attachments to his family, and is likely to become especially close to one person in particular—usually the person who feeds and trains him. However, it is important to be sure he does not become so reliant on that person's company that he becomes distressed if separated from them for only a minute.

Such a condition is called separation anxiety and, although the causes and cures can be complex according to the dog's specific circumstances, prevention is relatively straightforward; the dog should learn from a young age to be confident in his own company, and that you *always* come back.

If you have crate-trained your Rottie from when he was a puppy (see Chapter Two), it will make this training much simpler, as he will be confident in his crate and should view it as a safe, secure den.

- Do not spend all day, every day with your Rottweiler. Put him in his crate—in another room—for half an hour in the morning and evening.
- If he barks in his crate, never return to him. If you do, he will learn that when he "calls,"

Your Rottweiler must learn to accept periods of separation without becoming overanxious.

you come. So whenever you are gone, he'll bark and bark and bark.

- Only return when he is quiet, and be cheerful and loving to him. Never shout at him for barking earlier—he'll think you are angry that he was quiet!

- Before you put him in the crate and leave, do not make a big fuss over him. Matter-of-factly put him in the crate and leave. If you make a dramatic exit, giving lots of cuddles and kisses before leaving, it will make your dog miss you even more when you are gone.

If your Rottie wasn't brought up in a crate, teach him to love it! Bedding and chew toys will help him to enjoy himself in one. Do not expect too much too soon. Put him in the crate for only a few minutes at a time at first, gradually

making it longer the more comfortable he becomes. When he is happy in his crate, walk out of the room for just 30 seconds, then walk back in. Over a period of time, gradually wait longer before returning to him. As before, never return when he is anxious, only when he is calm.

The above methods should help to prevent separation problems. If your dog is suffering from the condition (he may be destructive and distressed when you leave a room), you should consult a professional dog behaviorist.

NEUTERING

If you do not intend to breed or show your dog, you should seriously consider having your Rottie neutered. This operation means your dog will not be able to reproduce. It is a routine procedure, in which the testicles are removed in a male, and the uterus and ovaries in a female. Like all operations, it does have its risks, but in a healthy animal, these are minimal.

Behavior

Your dog can reach sexual maturity from the age of four months on, though it is usually between six and twelve months (females can be as late as two years of age in rare instances).

A dog's powerful instincts to reproduce can cause many headaches for pet owners. When a female has a season, she will become irresistible to males, and will have to be kept away from them for up to three weeks. Unplanned litters can result, meaning you will have to cope with a pregnant female, raise the pups, and find good homes for them. This can be particularly difficult if the pups are nonpedigree.

Unneutered males have a tendency to roam, and many are lost or killed in road accidents when pursuing the scent of a female in heat. Intact (uncastrated) males may be territorial and aggressive to other dogs. They may also be prone to mounting, and excessive howling and barking.

Health

Along with behavioral advantages, sterilization has significant health benefits. Sterilized animals will not suffer from testicular tumors, and have a greatly reduced chance of developing protracted life-threatening prostate, mammary, and uterine cancers. Your veterinarian will be able to discuss the health benefits with you in more detail.

Disadvantages

Sterilization can have its disadvantages. Females in particular may have a tendency to put on weight, but this can be prevented by making sure your Rottie receives the correct diet and exercise. Coat changes can occur in some sterilized animals. In some cases, incontinence may result, but such instances are relatively rare.

If you are not planning to breed your Rottie, it is worth giving serious consideration to neutering.

After all the highs and lows of adolescence, you are ready to enjoy the relative calm of life with an adult Rottie.

When?

To avoid unwanted puppies being born, some rescue organizations have an early-neutering policy, where dogs are sterilized at 12 weeks of age, sometimes earlier. In responsible homes, where the veterinarian knows the owners will supervise their pets closely, it is not usually necessary for the operation to be performed this early, and most dogs are sterilized at around six months of age.

Contrary to popular belief, there is no need to let a female have one litter prior to being spayed, nor even one season before having her spayed.

Different veterinarians have their own views on the optimum time for sterilizing your Rottie. Ask the advice of your veterinarian; he will be able to discuss the pros and cons with you in more detail and will be able to advise you on what is best for your individual dog.

CHAPTER FOUR

THE FAMILY DOG

He may not be the obvious choice when it comes to choosing a family pet, but the highly adaptable and devoted Rottweiler will fit in well with families of most types.

The breed's intelligence means that there are all sorts of games and sports that you can teach your Rottweiler, and his love of walks will keep you both fit (see Chapter Five for details of fun, rewarding training activities).

A well-trained Rottweiler will be a wonderful addition to most families. He is loyal and loving, and enjoys sharing time with his human pack. Above all else, he is a fun dog, with a great sense of humor, that will bring smiles and laughter to your home.

However, if left unchecked, the Rottweiler's protective instincts can develop into a slight tendency to dominate the family. He may occasionally assert himself a little too

enthusiastically. But, all this can be avoided with the correct handling, training, and socialization from when he is a puppy, to be continued throughout his life (see Chapters Two and Three).

Right from day one, you should let your Rottie know that you are the boss. This does not mean that you should be cruel to him—apart from it being unkind, it is also unnecessary, as most Rotties will become incredibly stubborn if you try this tactic.

Instead, you should gently remind him that you are more important than he is. There is a variety of ways in which you can do this, such as making sure the family eats before he does, or preventing him from barging in front of people when walking through doors (see Chapter Three).

Rotties respond well to leadership, and your dog will respect your authority as long as it is kind, fair, and implemented consistently.

JINGLE BELLS

Pat and Les Price have owned Rottweilers for 30 years—raising their children alongside the dogs. Here, Pat recounts some of her own experiences.

"I have always been surrounded by animals, and cannot imagine life without them.

"My first Rottie was a lovely female called Jaega. Seven years later, my first daughter, Nicola, arrived. Jaega seemed to form an instant bond with her. She would sit for hours beside her carriage as if guarding her. Perhaps her protective and herding instincts were coming to the fore.

"There were no problems with jealousy from Jaega. Usually, dogs become jealous only if they are made to feel too important. Dogs are not children and they should not be treated as child substitutes. It is perfectly possible to love your dog and to treat him well, without having to pander to his every whim and produce a dog that is spoiled and uncontrollable.

"My second daughter, Shelley, arrived two years after Nicola, and Jaega was just as affectionate and protective of her. Frith, and, later on, Snoody, joined the family.

"My dogs have always been part of the family, but were given their limits, which were kept. As a result, I've never had any behavioral problems with them, and they have all been as good as gold around my children, who have grown up with Rottweilers.

"I remember, during the winter when we had snow, we would all go up to the woods. One year, we harnessed the dogs to a sleigh, and they pulled Nicola and Shelley around. They loved it, and it's become something of a family tradition.

"I would have no hesitation in saying that Rottweilers make suitable family pets. I would never have brought up my children among them if I thought differently. I remember my mother, who *did* have reservations about Rotties and kids being together, coming around and being very quickly converted. Most dogs make good family pets, just as long as their owners use some common sense."

ROTTWEILER RESCUE

The rescue dog is usually a good choice for someone who does not want the inconvenience and the sleepless nights that usually accompany a puppy. These little bundles of fur may be fun, but they can also wreak havoc.

A recently retired couple, who have some previous experience with dog ownership, and who now have the time to devote to the care of an adult Rottweiler, may be an ideal choice. They have the time, the experience, and the care, but they are not at the age where they want to be on their hands and knees clearing up "accidents."

Facts and Fiction

Unfortunately, the number of Rottweilers ending up at rescue shelters is increasing. Chris Tate, a trustee for the Rottweiler Welfare Association, has noticed a big increase over the last 15 years. "When I first started working with rescued Rotts, we had perhaps eight dogs a

*Through no fault of their own, too many
Rottweilers end up in rescue shelters.*

year," she says. "Nowadays we are rehoming
hundreds within the same timeframe."

Dogs can end up in rescue centers for all sorts
of reasons:

- **Indiscriminate breeding.** This produces
  dogs with poor temperaments and significant
  health problems that soon end up in rescue
  centers. Of course, this should in no way
  reflect upon the responsible breeders who
  care passionately about the welfare of
  their dogs.

- **Fear.** Past media coverage has left many
  people with a blackened impression of the
  breed. This has led to many owners
  abandoning their Rottie at the first signs of
  aggression, while others have been
  discouraged from rescuing a Rottie because
  they fear the breed can be aggressive.

- **Divorce.** This usually results in a change of
  lifestyle—one with little room for a Rottweiler.

- **Allergies.** An increasing number of animals
  are placed in rescue shelters for this reason.

- **Unemployment.** The daily feeding costs and
  annual veterinary fees can be expensive once
  a regular salary is no longer forthcoming.

Surprisingly few Rotties end up at shelters
because they have nasty tempers and cannot be
controlled.

Words of Warning

- Rescue centers are not an alternative means
  of acquiring a pedigree Rottweiler. Any
  money saved on purchase costs will
  eventually be spent on food, toys, bedding,
  and regular veterinary bills.

- A rescue Rottie requires a great deal of
  patience and kindness from his new owner.

- Some dogs—through no fault of their
  own—may have significant behavioral
  and/or physical problems. You may need to
  take your Rottie to a dog behaviorist.

- Your rescued pet may need a lot more
  attention from the veterinarian than other
  Rotties. Be prepared for the extra costs that
  will result.

It's not all gloom and doom, though. If, after
taking all of the above points into account, you
are still determined to go ahead, you are likely
to be highly rewarded. Given time, your dog
will probably become a devoted companion to
you, and you will have the added satisfaction of
knowing that you have given one animal a
much better life.

Top Tips For Success
Do
- Research the breed thoroughly.
- Give consistent discipline.
- Learn about "canine psychology."
- Make sure you can afford a dog.
- Make sure there is someplace nearby where you can exercise your Rottie regularly.

- Be prepared to give your dog time, time, and yet more time.

Don't
- Underestimate the everyday costs.
- Take on a rescue dog if you do not have the patience or commitment to deal with one.
- Forget about your neighbors—your Rottie may bark a lot when you first get him.

THE TATE GALLERY OF DOGS

Rescue worker Chris Tate has been working for the Rottweiler Welfare Association for more than 12 years. Unable to resist the appeal of the Rottweiler, Chris has taken on many herself.

"I've adopted quite a few rescue dogs over the years. One of my first was an eight-month-old female named Kelly. She was brought in by a woman who had bought the Rott for her brother a month earlier. The brother wanted to use Kelly as a guard dog, but she was too petrified of everything and everyone to be of any use.

"Kelly was an appalling sight when they brought her in. Some time in her past, her face had been horrifyingly disfigured. It was so bad that her jaw had been broken, and her whole face was

Kelly at the helm.

misshapen. The veterinarian checked her over and said that her injuries were consistent with being badly kicked in the face. To make matters worse, instead of being taken to a veterinarian for proper treatment, someone had tried to carry out their own makeshift repair job on her face.

"I was absolutely horrified that the poor thing had gone through so much, and was determined that she should be well looked after from then on. I knew that her face would probably deter potential owners, so I decided to take her myself.

"Once she was being properly treated, Kelly recovered remarkably well. Apart from her appalling facial injuries, very little remained of the poor little wretch I had taken in. She eventually died at the ripe old age of

12 years and 10 months. Between the time we took her in as an eight-month-old and the time she died, Kelly became a happy, lively, and much-loved member of our family, although, even to the end, she still hated all men. She would tolerate my husband but would pointedly ignore every other man.

"Another wonderful dog I had was Toddy Tate. A Rottweiler owner had seen Todd wandering around an area of woodland. Todd had a half-paralyzed face as a result of his collar getting caught on a tree branch somewhere in the woods.

"Kelly and Todd hit it off right away. Just like Kelly, Todd's face was a bit crooked, because of the paralysis, and his nose was a bit skewed to the right. I thought I'd have to keep him. Kelly and he made such a pair—'My pair of bookends,' I used to call them.

"After Kelly and Todd, I rescued several more Rotts: Max, Mackeson, and Guinness.

"Mack is probably my most successful rescue dog to date. Although he had a better start in life than many rescue dogs, he had been neglected. Nevertheless, he made a complete recovery, which just goes to show that a rescue dog can adapt to a new life and make a wonderful pet. Since I've had Mack, he's gone from strength to strength.

Mack—a favorite with the children.

"One year, I took Mack to a children's pet show, as an exhibit. There were all sorts of exotic animals there, from snakes to birds of prey. Despite this amazing display of animals, all the kids made a beeline for Mack, and he loved every minute of it. One child fell completely in love with Mack, draping himself around Mack's neck like a leech. Mack, for his part, tolerated all the (rather choking) cuddles and complete mayhem, without batting an eyelid.

"Because he is so wonderful with kids, and has such a great temperament, I decided to register him as a therapy dog. I take him along to visit children's groups and senior citizens' homes—people who would otherwise have little contact with pets of any description. One regular haunt of mine and Mack's is a nursing home. The people there love having a dog to pet. Many of them had dogs before, and Mack goes a little way toward making up for that lack of canine companionship. He is always made very welcome there, and I have never received any comments about him being an 'aggressive Rottweiler' or anything.

"Mack's great strength is that, somehow, he seems to have this instinctive ability to understand how people are feeling. If there was anyone who was very sad, he would always go straight to them, in a bid to cheer them up."

CARING FOR THE ADULT ROTTWEILER

After all the effort you have expended on caring for, training, and socializing your Rottweiler puppy, you should have a happy, well-adjusted, and healthy dog. However, it is important not to make the mistake of believing that now that your Rottie is an adult, things will largely take care of themselves. There are a number of routine tasks that must be carried out if you are going to keep your Rottie in tip-top condition.

Feeding

All dogs love food, and the Rottie is no exception. If he thinks he can get away with it, he will eat as much food as you can give him. It is important to remember that overfeeding is as cruel, and as potentially damaging to health, as underfeeding.

Strictly speaking, a Rottweiler should need only one meal a day. However, many owners prefer to give the daily allowance in two portions. Whichever feeding regime you decide on, make sure you stick to it, and that you are not tempted to give in to your Rottie's endearing requests for extra food.

Types of Food

There is a bewildering array of food products available for dogs. In most cases, the most sensible action is to stick to the diet plan given to you by the dog's breeder, previous owners, or rescue staff. If you did not receive a diet plan, get in touch with your veterinarian, who will be only too happy to advise you on the correct food type, quantity, and frequency of feeding.

Feeding Problems

As long as your adult Rottweiler remains healthy, you are unlikely to face any difficulties when feeding him. However, if problems *do* occur, try the following solutions:

- Take your dog to the veterinarian before embarking on any further action in order to rule out the possibility that your Rottie is ill.
- Find out if your Rottie is a "fussy eater." Some Rottweilers can become incredibly picky during adolescence, with a very small minority continuing this trend into their adult life. If this applies to your Rottie, you need to worry only if his choice of food is not giving him all the necessary nutrients.
- If your dog is reluctant to eat, try changing his routine. Some animals suddenly discover a renewed interest in food when their eating location is changed.
- Another tactic is to feed your reluctant eater alongside another dog—one with a healthy appetite. This usually results in your dog wolfing down his food.
- If you need to change your Rottie's diet, introduce the new food gradually, by adding a little of the new product to your dog's normal meal. Over time, increase the proportion of the new food.

Weight

There is a noticeable difference between male and female Rottweilers, not only in terms of weight, but also in overall build. It is important to remember that every dog is an individual, but, generally speaking, a male in top condition

There is considerable weight variation between a male and a female.

should weigh about 110 pounds (50 kg), while a female should weigh about 93 pounds (42 kg).

While some variation outside this weight range is perfectly acceptable, try not to let your Rottie put on too much weight. Just as in humans, obesity among dogs causes heart problems and aggravates joints. Stick to your feeding plan, and reward good behavior with a game rather than with an extra meal or treats.

Exercise

The Rottweiler was bred for a working life, and it is unfair to give him insufficient exercise. Two walks a day, of between one and two miles each, is what the caring Rottweiler owner should aim for.

Exercise plays a vital part in keeping your Rottie's mind active, as well as keeping his body healthy. Rottweilers can become bored and

frustrated very easily. It is the owner's responsibility to make sure this does not happen by taking the dog out for a walk every single day— bad-weather days and Christmas included!

Safety First

It is always advisable to keep your dog on a leash whenever you are out in a public place. This is for two main reasons:

- While your dog is on a leash, you have far more control over which members of the public he has contact with. Some people are afraid of large dogs, but if yours is on a lead, they will have no reason to be. If any members of the public do try to pet your dog, you can rest assured that your well-socialized Rottie will behave in a model fashion.
- Although the Rottie is, by nature, an obedient dog, it is amazing how a rabbit or a female in season can suddenly bring on a case of temporary deafness! The last thing any owner wants is to lose their dog or for him to run into the street.

If you dislike the idea of restricting your dog's freedom, try using an extendible leash. This allows your dog considerable freedom of movement, but leaves you in ultimate control.

If you are lucky enough to be able to take your Rottie somewhere where you have no worries about other people, other dogs, or traffic accidents, and you decide to let him run free, please remove his collar. Far too many animals are choked, or have accidents, because

EXERCISING YOUR ROTTWEILER

The Rottie is an active breed, and regular exercise will keep him fit and healthy.

of a collar getting caught on a branch. For this reason, it is a good idea to have your dog microchipped or tagged, just in case the worst happens and he does become lost.

Town or Country?

In an ideal world, all dog owners would live in the country, and have access to acres of interesting land in which their dogs can run, sniff, and play. However, there is no reason why a Rottweiler cannot live perfectly happily in a city. It is the amount of exercise that is the most important thing.

One of the beneficial side effects of city living is that frequent walking on concrete will wear down your Rottie's nails, thus reducing the need for clipping. If you live in the country, try to include regular walks on hard surfaces for this very purpose.

Wherever you live, and wherever you walk, remember to take along a poop scoop and plastic bags. It is only fair to clean up your dog's mess and so let other people enjoy the same walk.

Grooming

Rottweilers have short coats, making them one of the easier breeds to care for. Nevertheless, it is still a good idea to give a thorough brushing through your Rottie's coat once or twice a week. Not only does this remove dirt, etc., but it also means your Rottweiler is regularly handled.

The Rottweiler has a double coat, so it is important to buy a grooming brush and comb

The Rottweiler has a low-maintenance coat that is easy to care for.

that will comb both coats at the same time. You should start on your Rottie's head, and gradually work your way back. Include the legs and underbelly as you go along, eventually working your way back to the tail.

The Rottweiler sheds his coat twice a year, depending on the weather. When this happens he will need more regular grooming, using a fine-toothed comb, to loosen and remove the dead undercoat.

Bathing

Dogs do not dislike water, which is why bath-time should be an enjoyable experience rather than an awful chore. There will always be some dogs that, for no apparent reason, dislike being bathed, and others for whom the addition of shampoo is enough to send them running for cover. However, for many dogs, fear or dislike of the bath is simply a matter of insufficient familiarization. If your puppy is used to being in the bathtub (regardless of whether or not there is any water in it), bathtime should pose no problems.

On average, your adult Rottie will need a bath once every two to three months. This may increase during the winter months, when he may get muddier than normal, and also through the summer, when the war with fleas is really waged. Using a specially formulated anti-insecticidal shampoo will further help to keep fleas under control.

There are all sorts of dog shampoos available, catering to all budgets. Make sure that you do not use any form of detergent, or human shampoo, as this can encourage skin problems.

When you bathe your Rottie:

- Use a rubber mat so that he does not slip in the bath and injure himself.
- Make sure the water is lukewarm. Your dog will not be overly appreciative of cold water, and hot water will burn him.
- Wet and rinse your dog using a shower appliance. Not only is it easier, but it is also more effective at rinsing away the suds, thus avoiding skin problems.
- After his bath, give your Rottie a thorough rubdown with an absorbent towel. If it is extremely cold, you can use a hairdryer on moderate heat, so that he does not catch a chill.

Ear Care

The Rottweiler's ears should lie flat and close to the cheeks, so air does not circulate as easily in them as in breeds with upright, pricked ears. For this reason, you will need to check your Rottie's ears regularly for signs of infection, and to make sure there are no mites or an undue amount of wax.

If you have any worries, consult your veterinarian, who will be able to treat any infections, and can show you how to clean your dog's ears properly. *Never, ever,* use cotton swabs. You may cause serious damage to your Rottie's ears. If you buy an ear-cleaner product, follow the instructions on the packaging extremely carefully.

Tooth Care

If left unchecked, tooth decay and tartar can lead to a host of problems for your dog. A frequent result of poor dental care is gum disease. Not only is this painful, but it may also result in the complete loss of teeth.

Regular brushing will prevent tartar accumulation on the teeth.

Regular brushing is one of the main preventive measures. You can use either a fingerbrush or a toothbrush, combined with a meat-flavored toothpaste designed for dogs. Alternatively, there are numerous chews available that are actively supposed to prevent the buildup of tartar on the teeth, as well as helping to break down any existing tartar.

Give your Rottie plenty of chew bones, marrowbones, and sturdy toys. By chewing regularly on these, he will develop strong teeth and jaws. A regular check by your veterinarian will also ensure that your dog maintains good dental hygiene.

If the nails do not wear down naturally, they will need to be trimmed.

Nail Care

Check your Rottie's nails regularly. Nails that are too long may indicate that your Rottie is not walking enough on hard surfaces. Or it may be that his nails are not growing at the angle necessary to become worn down naturally.

If you decide to trim your Rottie's nails yourself, make sure the correct clippers are used, such as a pair of guillotine nail clippers. Never cut off too much at a time, or you may cut into the "quick" of your dog's nail—the nail's nerves and the blood supply. If nicked, this area can become very painful and possibly infected. If bleeding does occur, apply a styptic substance to stop the blood.

If you are in any doubt about how to trim your Rottie's nails, ask a veterinarian to show you the correct procedure.

Fleas and Worms

Every owner should treat his or her dog with some sort of regular flea treatment. This can take the form of drops deposited on the skin/coat, or collars, or orally digested pills. Bathing with anti-insecticidal shampoos can also help. Regularly wash and vacuum your dog's bedding and favorite spots in the home to avoid reinfestation.

As an adult, your Rottweiler should be wormed regularly. Your veterinarian will be able to advise you on a suitable worming program. Whichever product you choose, be sure to follow the instructions very carefully.

Veterinary Checks

A healthy Rottweiler should not need to visit the veterinarian more than once a year. A good time to make this once-yearly visit is when your Rottie receives his annual booster inoculations.

However, if at any time you have concerns about the health of your dog, then please take him to your veterinarian.

SENIOR CARE

Rotties are robust, healthy dogs whose hardiness can help them breeze through their senior years with few signs of deteriorating health. For some, the only sign of advancing age is a few gray hairs on the chin and a greater love of home comforts. Other dogs may suffer possible health problems and character changes.

Exercise and Food

Some venerable Rotties continue to expend as much energy as when they were puppies, but most will start to slow down, wanting to spend more time indoors, and more time sleeping or lounging in a comfy bed in a warm spot inside the house.

As he becomes less active, you should become more flexible in your exercise regimes. Listen to your dog and let him choose his own level—he will tell you when he has had enough or if he doesn't want to go out. The older dog usually prefers a couple of gentle, short strolls to anything too strenuous. If you have younger dogs, you may want to consider walking them separately. A proud, stubborn Rottie will desperately try to keep up with his juniors, and may strain himself in the process.

If your Rottweiler is exercising less, he won't need as much food. Most Rotties will try to convince you otherwise, but don't give in. Obesity is detrimental to a dog's health

Respond to the changing needs of your Rottie as he gets older.

at the best of times, but in an elderly dog it can be fatal, putting excessive pressure on the heart.

Rotties rarely lose their appetite, although there may be partial loss of smell and taste. If an oldie starts picking at his food, it is usually a sign that something is wrong, and a veterinarian should be consulted. The dog's diet may need to be adapted as he ages. Most dogs require a diet that is lower in protein. Many food manufacturers now produce foods especially designed for the older dog. Also, be aware of how much your Rottie is drinking. Increased thirst can denote health problems.

Routine Care

When you give your Rottie his once-weekly grooming, run your hands over his body to check for injuries or suspicious-looking lumps. Cancer is the big killer in the breed, although, if it is caught early enough, it can often be successfully treated. If, when grooming your dog, you find anything that worries you, consult your veterinarian.

You should also pay particular attention to your Rottie's nails and teeth. Your Rottweiler's dental regime should be as rigorous as ever, while nails should be checked more regularly. They may not wear down so easily if he is exercising less. Don't forget the dewclaws— they could curl around and start digging into the dog.

Character Changes

Character-wise, an aged Rottweiler may become a little grumpier and more reclusive. If you have a lot of visitors, he will probably want to take himself off to a quiet corner somewhere, rather than revel in the company, as he may have done in his youth.

If you have a younger dog, or a puppy, always supervise the two of them. Your oldie will want to take life at his own pace, and may become intolerant toward a youngster that keeps pestering him to play. There are only so many times that even the most accepting of dogs will allow their tails to be chewed! Watch both dogs carefully to make sure tempers do not flare. If your youngster is getting too boisterous, separate the dogs to give your oldie a much-needed rest. By contrast, some older dogs love having a puppy around; it seems to give them a new lease on life.

EUTHANASIA

One of the saddest aspects of owning a dog is knowing that he will die. While there is little you can do to stop this, you do have the power to allow your Rottie to die peacefully and with dignity. If he is in pain, has very little quality of life, and the veterinarian has informed you that there is nothing more he can do, please do not let your Rottie suffer. As his owner, and having spent many years with him, you will know when the time has come to say good-bye.

Euthanasia is painless, and works by putting your dog into a deep sleep, from which he will never wake. If your Rottie has a fear of the veterinarian, or you simply don't want his last moments to be spent in a veterinary clinic, some veterinarians are quite happy to make home visits under such circumstances.

Once your Rottie has passed away, there are several options available to you. Some people choose to cremate their pet, which allows them to scatter his ashes in a favorite spot, or along a much-loved walk. Or you can bury him in a special pet cemetery, or allow your veterinarian to dispose of the body for you.

All pet owners feel the loss of their beloved animals dearly. However, if you feel particularly distressed, you may find it helpful to talk to someone. Your veterinarian will be very supportive, and probably refer you to a pet-bereavement counselor. Other people, who have lost their own pets, may also be able to offer you help, sympathy and support, and, if all else fails, a therapist may be able to help you come to terms with your loss.

TIME TO LET GO

Teresa and Trevor Killick have kept Rottweilers for many years. Their first Rottie, Ch. Pendley Goldfinch (Travis), died relatively young, at the age of eight. Teresa recalls how she and Trevor reached the difficult decision to put Travis to sleep.

"I've had dogs since I was 12. Trevor and I originally kept German Shepherd Dogs, but Trevor had always fancied a Rottie, so we decided to get one.

"After being thoroughly evaluated, we eventually got Pendley Goldfinch. Travis was bought as a pet, but he was so handsome we ended up presenting him at shows. He did well—winning Best of Breed at Crufts, the world's largest dog show, held in England. We retired Travis at the age of six. He had an excellent career, we had a wonderful Rottie, and we all had a wonderful life together—he was everything you could wish for in a dog.

"However, when he was seven years old, Travis tripped on the stairs and hurt his leg. He couldn't put any weight on it, and the scream he made when he fell down the stairs was very unnerving.

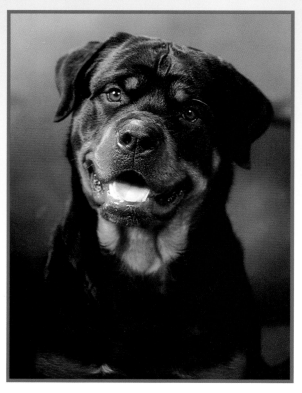

Travis: The caring owner must decide when it is time to let go.

"After various X-rays and other investigations, we realized that the fall had virtually shattered his leg. There was hardly any bone left, and we had to make the decision to have his leg amputated. It was very, very hard.

"I think the amputation affected us more than it did Travis. He just seemed to get on with things. He had his own, unique style of locomotion, where his remaining back leg would move underneath his body, to balance him. He used it almost as we would a crutch. He still bounded across fields and dived into everything. Losing his leg in no way affected his quality of life.

"Travis had loved the show life so much that we wanted him to see another— amputated leg or not! We took him to a Club Championship show, and he wagged his stump all the way there. He knew we were taking him to a show and he was *so* excited.

"When we took Travis into the ring, and the judge listed his previous titles and the story behind his missing limb, there wasn't a dry eye in the house. Travis loved the whole experience, knowing that all attention was focused on him, and played up to the crowd shamelessly. Just before he exited the ring we took a lap of honor. Travis shot round that ring! I swear that, despite his missing leg, he was the fastest dog at that show. He left the ring to a standing ovation.

"Travis went from strength to strength after that show, having a very successful career as a stud dog. He became famous the world over, and his progeny are also going on to achieve great success. He made us so proud, but I always tell people that he was bought as a pet first and foremost—his show successes were incidental. No amount of money could replace the memories that he has left us with, and we both count ourselves as incredibly lucky to have had the privilege of owning such a dog.

"Because Travis was such a wonderful pet, making the decision to put him to sleep was one of the hardest, most awful experiences of our lives. It was heartbreaking. A year after his amazing reception at the Club show, Travis collapsed into a coma, brought on as a result of kidney failure. We tried hard to save him, trying to induce him out of his coma. We succeeded, but it was clear that he was in unimaginable, agonizing pain. Trevor and I talked it over—between ourselves and with our supportive veterinarian. The decision to euthanize Travis was the only one open to us, really, if we weren't going to let him suffer.

"Part of you, deep down, knows if the time has come—when enough's enough—and postponing death is a form of cruelty. I always think that we are incredibly lucky to be able to end the suffering of our pets, which is more than can be said for humans.

"What you really have to look for is your pet's enjoyment in life. As long as our Rotties have bright eyes, are eating, are interested in what's going on, and are able to get around, I'll fight with them all the way to let them live. But once it's clear that they're suffering, that they've lost their dignity, are in excruciating pain, or just don't care anymore, it's time to let go.

"I'd advise anyone going through a similar experience to talk things through. It always helps to have someone to talk to, to understand and to help you. Veterinarians are usually very sympathetic, and will really support you if you decide to put an animal to sleep. Of course, it's still your decision—no one can make it for you, and it's a real shame that our pets can't just die in their sleep. But they don't. I was devastated when we lost Travis, but, looking back, it helps to know that I'd relieved Travis of that awful suffering at the end.

"We've had many wonderful Rotties since then, although Travis will always occupy a special place in our hearts. Unfortunately, it seems the decision to euthanize is soon going to be ours to make again. We have the most beautiful 12-year-old male Rottie at the moment, Travillons Dare Devil. He is crippled with arthritis, and suffers real pain some days. We won't let him go just yet as most of the time he is pain free, contented, and still showing a zest for life. However, we know the time will come, before too long, when that won't always be the case. It *will* be awful, but we will *not* let our Rotties suffer. They have been such faithful and loving companions to us, it's the least we can do."

CHAPTER FIVE

BROADENING HORIZONS

Although originally bred as a working animal, today's Rottie still possesses all the natural instincts of his ancestors. He needs plenty of exercise, both mental and physical, to keep him happy and healthy. The average Rottweiler will thrive if basic training is extended.

CITIZENSHIP

The "Good Citizen" programs are excellent starting places if you want to take your Rottie's initial training further. The American Kennel Club's Good Citizen Program and the British Kennel Club's Good Citizen Dog Scheme aim to encourage responsible pet ownership and to educate dog owners about the benefits of having a well-behaved pet.

The programs test a dog's ability to behave in a calm, confident manner in a variety of different situations, including:

- Walking on a loose leash in a controlled manner
- Walking through a crowd
- Being approached and petted by a stranger
- Meeting another dog
- Being handled and groomed
- Responding to a number of basic commands.

There are many training clubs in the U.K. and the U.S. that take part in the programs and offer courses to prepare your dog for the tests. To find out more, contact your national kennel club.

COMPETITIVE OBEDIENCE

In British Obedience, considerable emphasis is placed on heelwork, whereas American Obedience has a wider range of exercises, many of which are found in British Agility and Working Trials. As a result, two distinct trends have developed. In Britain, the Border Collie is definitely the king of the Obedience ring; in the U.S., the variation in exercises has allowed other breeds to excel. Rottweilers tend to do well in American Obedience because of the importance placed on events such as tracking and retrieving.

Getting Started

Rottweilers, being intelligent and adaptable dogs, seem to enjoy Obedience, but remember that they can also become bored very quickly. Try to begin each training session with a game so that your Rottie learns to associate Obedience with fun. Also, make each training session different from the one before; variety is the key to successful training.

Simple step-by-step instructions for *recall, retrieve,* and *heeling* are given below, as a way of finding out whether Obedience is right for you. If you want to find out more about Obedience and how to take part, contact your national kennel club for details of classes in your area.

AGE LIMITS

Remember: both the KC and the AKC will only allow animals over six months old to participate in Obedience.

The Recall

Rottweilers have a strong desire for human companionship, and particularly enjoy the *recall* exercise. Basic *recall,* when the dog comes when called, can be taught when your Rottie is still a puppy (see page 35), but Obedience *recall* is a more advanced maneuver.

There are two types of *recall* in Obedience, the Novice *recall* and the Advanced *recall.* Only the Novice Recall is described here.

To complete the Novice Recall successfully, a dog must:
- Sit
- Wait
- Come
- Sit-front

Teaching the Novice Recall

- First, command your dog to *"Sit."* Then ask him to *"Wait"* or *"Stay."*
- Walk a few steps away, to the end of a loose lead.
- Recall your dog by calling *"Come"* or *"Heel."*
- As soon as he reaches you, use a treat to guide him into the *Sit-front* (the dog is right at your feet in a sitting position). His back should be straight and he should be directly facing you, not crooked in any way. His head should be held up at attention, ready to react to your next command.
- Give him the treat as soon as he responds correctly. In Obedience, the object of the exercise is for the dog to come to you as quickly as possible. By rewarding him each time he is successful, you are encouraging him to respond faster the next time.
- Repeat the above until your Rottie has mastered the exercise. Then progress to teaching him to *Sit-front* on your left or right, using different commands for each side.

As you become more experienced, you can vary direction and pace in heeling, and perhaps practice with the dog on your right side as well as your left.

Heeling

Your Rottweiler should walk on your left side in a calm, consistent manner, neither in front of you nor behind, but directly at your side.

Whereas the agile, quick Border Collie is able to respond to signals very quickly, the Rottie can take some time to readjust his position. To overcome this problem, many Rottweiler handlers prefer to teach heeling using the "on the leg" method, which requires the dog to rest his head on the handler's leg or knee. This keeps the Rottie's position constant, and alerts him sooner to the handler's intention to change direction.

- Begin with a game to get your Rottie's attention. When he is fully alert, position him correctly on your left side with his head resting lightly on your leg.
- Initially, practice the *heel* position while remaining stationary. Walking can wait until you are both more accomplished.
- Hold a toy in your right hand. Make sure that your Rottie is focusing on the toy, and try to hold your position for a few moments.
- Repeat the above steps on several occasions. With each practice session increase the length of time your Rottie has to stand *at heel*.
- Raise your hand closer to your face with each session, so that your dog becomes accustomed to looking at your face and hand for his signal. Reward him if he does this correctly.
- When he has mastered the *heel* position and you have his undivided attention, walk in a clockwise circle. This maneuver is the easiest of the *heel* moves, and will teach your Rottie how to stay *at heel* when on the move.
- As you get better, you can progress to turns and changes of direction and pace.

GOOD GOLLY MISS MOLLY

Caroline Lee's first Rottie, Molly, was such an intelligent dog it was soon apparent that she would need a hobby to keep her amused.

"Right from the start it was clear that Molly was going to be a star," says Caroline. "She was extremely intelligent and game for anything. I have always believed that training should begin right from the moment you bring a dog home, so, while Molly was only eight weeks old, I introduced her to Obedience. She took to it like a duck to water.

"The golden rule in Obedience is to get your dog's attention. It's the first thing they teach you in classes. I began my attention training with Molly just by taking her with me everywhere and talking to her constantly. As a puppy, she loved the sound of my voice and gave me her full attention. I think it was reassuring for her. I haven't lost her concentration even though she's now fully grown.

"I trained Molly using her leash as her reward. This might sound boring, but I tried to use it as I would a

Molly loves the challenge of Competitive Obedience.

toy, so that Molly had lots of fun with it. Molly always associates her leash with a good time, and, unlike treats or other toys, I can take it into the Obedience ring. Molly has her reward right there, in front of her, the whole time, so, unlike some dogs, she doesn't forget everything she's learned once the toys are out of sight.

"As a Rottweiler, Molly's main strengths are *scent* and *recall*. In fact, I'm sure she thinks she's a retriever. She retrieves the mail and the paper every morning, and, if you accidentally drop anything, Molly will always pick it up and return it to you.

"I don't think Molly will ever live out a quiet retirement. She's always on the go doing something. One of her great strengths is her versatility—Molly has done so much. As well as Obedience and Carting, Molly has also appeared on the show circuit, recently winning a Best in Show. One of the things I'm most proud of, though, is her work as a therapy dog. This gives Molly a chance to show how sweet-natured, loyal, gentle, and affectionate she can be."

CANINE FREESTYLE

Canine Freestyle, or Heelwork to Music, is an offshoot of Competitive Obedience, where the dog and handler perform dance-oriented footwork in time to the music, rather than the traditional heeling exercises of Obedience.

A relatively new sport, Freestyle is increasing rapidly in popularity, particularly in the United States, although the American Kennel Club has yet to give the sport official recognition. However, there are numerous clubs and associations all over the world that put on Freestyle shows.

There are two types of dog dancing: Canine Freestyle, where creativity is considered most important; and U.S. Canine Freestyle, which is more like Obedience but is set to music. Performances can last anywhere between three and six minutes. Ring size varies according to venue, although the average is about 40 feet by 80 feet (12 m by 24 m).

Performance and Competition

Every organization has its own classes and points system, but most clubs award points for the following elements:

- Technical execution (i.e., difficulty of moves, precision, handling ability, and the dog's enthusiasm)
- Artistic impression (i.e., choreography, costume design, synchronization, and interpretation of the music)

Weaves

An impressive move, in which the dog weaves between your legs, this requires good coordination between dog and handler, particularly for a larger breed like the Rottweiler.

- Motivate your Rottie with a game.
- Stand with one leg in front of the other with your knees slightly bent. Make sure there is enough room for your dog to pass between your legs.
- Encourage your Rottie to move through the gap between your legs using a toy to guide him. Say *"Weave"* as he does so.
- Once he can do this, teach him how to do two weaves together. As soon as he has done the first, take a step forward, repositioning yourself so that your Rottie can go between your legs once more. Guide him through the same way as before.
- Keep practicing. Remove the toy, so that your Rottie needs only your hand to guide him, and eventually work up to a level where, following a vocal command alone, he can do several weaves in succession.

Top Tips

- Choose a piece of music that is catchy, and to which you can quite easily choreograph your routine.
- Choose costumes that are eye-catching and jaunty.
- Remember to smile—constantly—even when you are giving your Rottie commands. The ability to say your commands discreetly will give your performance a more seamless effect, and may earn you some extra points.

THE LAST WALTZ

Linda Toplis has been active in the world of Heelwork to Music since it began. Here she describes how she and her current dancing partner, Rory, got started.

"Before taking up Heelwork to Music, Rory and I competed in Obedience and Working Trials. Unfortunately, he developed a back problem that put an end to his career. After visiting a canine osteopath, we were assured that, as long as we were careful, Rory's back shouldn't prevent him from carrying out normal activities, so I decided to try him at Heelwork to Music. There are no set maneuvers in Heelwork to Music, which made it ideal, and Rory proved to be a natural.

"We always start off by playing several pieces of music, to see which one will work. I find that you never know which music is right until you try it out with your dog. Rory has his own input when choosing the music. If he doesn't like it, he'll walk off!

"Once we've decided on the music, I use clicker training to teach Rory the dance moves. The only thing with Rotties is that they have to want to do it. You'll never get anywhere by trying to bully them. Rory's so willing to learn new things that we can create whole routines before we know

Rory gets in some practice at home, hurdling Furnis.

it. He even invents a few moves of his own.

"Rory's biggest achievement to date is coming third in one event. Our performance was so well received that we were then invited to perform at a large show. The piece of music we danced to was the *Blue Danube*. A Rottweiler dancing away to a waltz is quite a sight!

"One of my favorite routines is *Rocking All Over The World* by Status Quo. We perform it like a '50s jive dance. I play the part of the man and Rory is the girl. I hold my hand out and he twirls (spins) around underneath it, and then goes between my legs. Rory loves that one. It seems to have stuck in his head. Recently, the song was played on the television and Rory came straight up to me and sat beside me in his start position, looking up at me as if to say, 'Well, come on. Let's get on with it!' We hadn't performed that routine for more than a year and a half!

"Rotties are excellent candidates for Heelwork to Music. They pick things up so quickly. Our other Rottie has never done anything more than basic training, but when I tried to do one of Rory's routines with her she had it very near perfect! She'd learned it all just from watching Rory."

AGILITY ABILITY

Agility can be enormous fun. It involves dogs of all breeds negotiating an obstacle course. The dog has to run a course within a set time and with no faults. The fastest clear round wins.

There are different types of Agility, based on the size of the dog. Rottweilers take part in Standard/Over 22 inches (56 cm) Agility, which will include the larger breeds such as German Shepherds, Border Collies, and Golden Retrievers.

AGE LIMITS

Overexerting your Rottie when he is a youngster is dangerous. Being such a large animal, the Rottweiler is particularly prone to damage to his joints and ligaments, and he needs time to mature fully before starting any physically strenuous event. Most kennel clubs impose an age limit of between one year and 18 months before a dog is permitted to enter Agility competitions.

Getting Started

As with any canine sport, good fitness is an essential prerequisite. It is worth taking your pet to your veterinarian to have him checked over first. Make sure that you are fit, too. Running around an Agility course with your Rottie can be very tiring!

You will need to contact your national kennel club for information about Agility clubs in your area. Some clubs may advertise their training courses on local bulletin boards.

Communication

Agility relies on a strong rapport between dog and handler. If your Rottie does not trust you, or does not respect your authority, you will never complete the course.

Body language plays a strong role. For example, your dog will take the direction in which you are running, or facing, as the direction in which you want him to go. He will also look to you for tacit approval before tackling an obstacle.

You will use verbal commands to communicate any other intentions to your Rottie. These commands are also used to help a dog avoid "traps." Traps are obstacles that are put in the course to test the handler's skills. Usually, they are placed in such a way as to make the dog think that they are part of the obstacle and should therefore be tackled. It is a real test of a handler's ability to steer the dog away from the trap and redirect him to the correct piece of equipment.

Teaching Commands

There are no rules about which commands should be used in Agility. Some common commands, which you might like to try with your Rottie, are listed below:

Directional Commands

DIRECTION	COMMAND
Left turn	*"Back"*
Right turn	*"Right"*
For the dog to be on your left	*"Heel"*
For the dog to be on your right	*"Richt"*

Commands Used to Negotiate Obstacles	
EQUIPMENT	COMMAND
Hurdles	*"Over"*
Long jump	*"Jump"*
Tire	*"Tire"*
Weave	*"Weave"*
Dog walk	*"Walk"*
A-frame	*"Ramp"*
Seesaw	*"Seesaw"*
Tunnel	*"Tunnel"*

Once you have decided which commands you are going to use, you need to teach them to your Rottie. Most Agility trainers use "Say as he does it" training. You encourage the dog to perform an action, and, while he does so, you repeat the command for it. It should not be too long before your Rottie associates the action with the command and can perform it on request.

The directional commands can be taught in a similar manner. With your Rottie seated next to you, throw a ball to your left or right. When your Rottie chases after it, call out the relevant command. He will soon learn the difference between his left and right.

Tackling the Obstacles

There are three main categories of obstacles in Agility: jumps, tunnels, and contact equipment.

Jumps

An Agility course contains a number of hurdles, a tire jump, and a long/broad jump. Jumping obstacles must be approached with care because Rottweilers can injure their joints through too hard an impact. The following method can be used to teach the hurdle jumps.

- Set up your hurdle so it is no more than a few inches/centimeters off the ground. Ask your Rottie to *"Sit"* and *"Stay"* in front of it.
- While he sits there, walk around to the other side of the hurdle and call him over.
- If he responds successfully, say *"Over"* as he jumps. Reward his success with a treat or with play.
- If your Rottie tries to run around the hurdle, attach his leash and repeat the above steps, using the leash to encourage him toward you over the hurdle.

A fit Rottie can clear jumps with ease.

- As your Rottie improves, gradually increase the height of the hurdle. For Rottweilers, the maximum height is 30 inches (76 cm) in the U.K., and 24 inches (61 cm) in the U.S.
- Discourage your Rottie from ducking underneath the hurdle by placing a pole across, barring his way.
- Once your Rottie is successfully jumping the hurdle at its maximum height, train him to jump several in succession.

Tunnels

Tunnels may not come as naturally to a Rottweiler as to a terrier, with his history of "going to ground." However, the ever-adaptable Rottie can learn to traverse the different tunnels very quickly, so long as his handler shows patience and provides plenty of reassurance.

There are two types of tunnel: the rigid/open tunnel, and the collapsible/closed tunnel.

The collapsible tunnel has no frame to keep it open. It is made of cloth and the dog has to push his way through it. As your Rottie will not be able to see where he is going, it is important to give him lots of reassurance.

- Fold the cloth back, so that the tunnel is short enough for your Rottie to see right through.
- Position your Rottie at the tunnel entrance, walk around to the other side, and encourage him through. If he does this, use your command word while he is inside.
- Fold down a little more of the tunnel and repeat the exercise, again rewarding him with lots of praise if he completes it successfully.

- Continue the exercise in stages, until your Rottie is confidently running through the maximum length of the tunnel: 120 inches (305 cm) in the U.K., and 180 inches (457 cm) in the U.S.

Contact Equipment

The contact equipment in Agility includes:
- The seesaw, which is much like a child's. The dog has to walk on at one end, balance in the middle, and then walk off at the other end.
- The A-frame, which is a steep-sided "A"-shaped ramp. The dog has to run up one side, and then run down the other. It has slats to help the dog maintain a grip.
- The dog walk. This is a narrow walkway, raised off the floor, with a ramp at the beginning and end.

Contact equipment is so called because the dog has to touch certain points of the obstacle—usually at the beginning and the end—before the exercise is considered successfully completed. In most cases, this is to prevent the dog from jumping onto an obstacle at the wrong point, or leaving an obstacle too soon, and possibly injuring himself (e.g., jumping off the A-frame from too high a position).

Contact obstacles are usually quite easy to teach because training is done with treats. A treat placed at a contact point is all the encouragement most dogs need to touch that spot routinely.

Build up the height of the A-frame so that your Rottweiler progresses with confidence.

The A-Frame

- Start off by placing the A-frame flat on the ground, so that it is just a horizontal board.
- With your Rottie next to you, encourage him to run the length of the frame. Say your command *"Ramp,"* and reward him when he reaches the end.
- Gradually raise the height of the equipment until it has reached a marked incline. Praise him each time he completes it.
- Place a treat at the beginning and end of the A-frame to make sure your Rottie touches the contact points.
- As the frame is raised higher, your Rottie will need more of a run-up to reach the top.

Weaving Poles

The weaving poles are separate from the other categories of obstacles. As the name suggests, they consist of a series of vertical poles through which the dog has to weave.

- Set up your line of poles so that they are at an angle of 45 degrees, rather than fully vertical. Alternate the poles, so that the first is set to a 45-degree angle to the left, the second is 45 degrees to the right, and so on.
- Position your Rottie so that the first pole is on his left.
- Use a treat to guide him through, saying *"Weave"* as you do so.
- As he becomes accustomed to the exercise and increases speed, you can raise the poles gradually upright, until they are eventually vertical.

And Finally...

With their working history, and their need for activity, most Rottweilers will love Agility, but remember:

- Never push too hard.
- Always make training sessions frequent but short.
- Always praise and reward your Rottie. Once you have lost his trust and motivation, it can be hard to regain it.

STEADY AS SHE GOES

Gladys Ogilvy-Shepherd has an unrivaled experience in Agility, particularly with Rottweilers.

"I took up Agility because I have strong feelings about Rottweilers. There's a lot more to a Rottie than simply looking pretty in the show ring! The Rottie is a working breed and should be kept active. Agility is a great way of doing this because it's so much fun!

"Rotties are great dogs to train—very steady, quick to learn, and easy to motivate. They may not be the fastest dogs around the course, but their steadiness makes up for it. Rotties don't waste time having to go back to an obstacle because they didn't finish it properly!

"If you're going to do Agility, it's worthwhile trying to get a dog from a working line. A working Rottie is an improvement in all sorts of ways including concentration, agility, stamina, motivation, speed, and versatility—all of which help in Agility.

"I do quite a lot of my training out on walks. I remember one funny occasion very well. One morning, when I had taken the dogs out for a walk, I decided to practice our *sits* and *stays*. There is an obstacle in Agility known as the Table. The dog has to jump onto the table, and sit or lie down for five

Gladys Ogilvy-Shepherd is a strong believer in giving Rottweilers work to do.

seconds. *Sits* and *stays* are very important for this obstacle.

"On the walk, I sat them all down, asked them to '*Sit*' and '*Wait*,' walked on by myself for a few yards, and then called them to '*Come*.' I think I got about a hundred yards further before I realized that my female Rottie, Glynette, wasn't with me. I had trained her to come only when I called, 'Glynette, *come*,' and of course, I had only called out '*Come*.' She was so obedient, bless her, that she was still sitting there, in the distance, patiently waiting for my next command. That's a Rottie for you. If you earn their loyalty, you have it for life.

"I think I'm probably getting too old for Agility now. It is definitely a sport for a young, fit person! Not so long ago, I entered one competition where the rules stated that, before you did the Table, you had to run two laps of the ring. The trouble was that the ring was enormous. By the time I had done my two laps and got Glynette to jump up on the table, I barely had the breath to tell her to '*Sit*' and '*Stay*.' I was utterly exhausted—it took quite a lot of brandy to restore me!

"I'll try to keep myself involved with Agility, though. If you've never tried it, you don't know what you're missing!"

FLYBALL

Flyball is a relay race for dogs. Usually, there are two competing teams, each containing four dogs (and their handlers). A dog is released from the starting line and has to race to the other end of the track to retrieve a tennis ball from the Flyball box. Once he has retrieved the ball, he has to race back to the starting line. As soon as he has crossed that line, another dog is released to run the course. The winning team is the one in which all four dogs have completed their run in the fastest time.

If a dog incurs any faults (e.g., if he does not leap every hurdle, or if he does not trigger the box), he must attempt the course again, after all the other team members have finished their runs.

Who Can Do Flyball?

Flyball is easy to learn, enormous fun, and great exercise. It is highly competitive, and requires the handlers and the dogs to work as part of a team. If this sounds like you and your Rottie, you should try Flyball—you'll probably love it.

Your level of involvement in Flyball is entirely up to you. While there are national competitions that are taken very seriously, there is no reason why you cannot stay at hobby level where competitiveness is outweighed by the emphasis on having a good time.

Teaching Flyball

Teaching Flyball relies mainly on your Rottweiler's interest in the tennis ball. Your Rottie *must* get excited by the prospect of getting a tennis ball at the end of the course, or he will not attempt to get that ball with the sense of urgency necessary for a successful Flyball competitor—it is a race, after all!

As an exceptionally quick learner, the Rottie should master most aspects of Flyball very quickly, but if he does not, do not despair—some dogs can take quite a long time to learn. If your Rottie shows no discernible interest, however, or if he is clearly unhappy with the game, do not force him to continue. Instead, give him a complete break from Flyball for a while, and come back to it later.

Operating the Flyball Box

Your club will teach your Rottie how to use their model. But

- You should accustom your dog to the sight and sound of the box. The Rottweiler is not a nervous breed, but some dogs can find the noise disturbing, not to mention the flying tennis balls appearing out of nowhere!

- Take your dog along to club sessions, sitting him reasonably close to the box. Over time, your Rottie will get used to seeing it operate, and will become desensitized to it.

Teaching the Hurdles

The height of the hurdles varies. In the U.K. 12 inches (30 cm) is standard, in the U.S. the height is variable and is determined by the smallest member of the team. The hurdles are designed to test the dog's accuracy, not his jumping ability (the hurdles are very low). Any dogs choosing to go around them, instead of over them, can lose a team the match.

- Teach your dog to jump these hurdles in the same way as in Agility (see page 76).
- Teach your dog to avoid avoidance! Reward him well every time he goes over a hurdle.

DIY FLYBALL

Obedience trainer Billy McWilliam describes here how he got started in Flyball.

"Many years ago, before Flyball had been heard of in the U.K., I bought an American book that described the sport. I thought, 'Hmm, that sounds interesting,' and decided to give it a go. Because the sport was so new, I couldn't get hold of a Flyball box, so I decided to make my own.

"I ended up with a creation that looked a little like a medieval trebuchet (catapult machine). It had some strange components: a ballcock from a toilet cistern, and a piece from a car hood! It was a strange-looking machine, but it worked brilliantly!

"My male, Duke, and my female, Elsa, were trained to use the box in no time. Rotties are naturally clever. I have a baby Rott at the moment and, although he's really too small to operate the box, he's

Duke: A natural at Flyball.

already grasped the principle behind it.

"I've done most Flyball with Duke—he was a tremendous dog. We never entered any competitions; instead, our team traveled around the country putting on demonstrations to raise money for charity. Duke was a winner with the crowd. As well as Flyball, we used to perform a trick where he jumped through a fiery hoop, which the crowds loved.

"Duke adored anything active. When we were performing Flyball demonstrations, and the box had run out of balls, it was hilarious to see my attempts to reload it. Duke loved the tennis ball flying at him so much that I would have to load the box one-handed, and use the other arm to hold him back. He wanted to press that pedal!

"I concentrate mainly on Obedience, now, but I'd recommend Flyball to anyone. It's a great sport, and I still have my first home-made box!"

SCENT HURDLING

Scent Hurdling is a variation on the Flyball course. As in Flyball, the dog has to run a course, jumping over four hurdles on the way. The main difference is that, instead of retrieving a tennis ball, the dog has to retrieve a dumbbell, using scent alone. The dog is expected to find his dumbbell and bring it back over the hurdles to the finishing line.

In place of the Flyball box there is a square platform, which is divided into four triangles—red, blue, green, and yellow. A dumbbell of the same color is placed on each section. To help the audience, each dog wears a scarf of the same color as the dumbbell.

Each time a dumbbell is taken, a dummy one is placed in its spot, so that each dog has a choice of four. The platform is turned a certain number of degrees each time, too, so the dog cannot memorize where his particular dumbbell is located.

THE WORKING ROTTWEILER

Most Rottweilers derive a great deal of satisfaction from a working lifestyle. Some of the working activities that you and your Rottie can try are listed below.

Herding

The Rottweiler's traditional working role as a herding animal means that most Rotties love this activity.

To date, there is little in the way of Rottweiler-herding training and competition across the globe. There are sheep trials, but the traditional method of working sheep is different to the gathering and herding style of the Rottie. The British Kennel Club offers no formal herding tests and the American Kennel Club introduced Herding Tests and Herding Trials only as recently as 1994.

Herding Tests are far less competitive than Herding Trials, and tend to be used as the beginner's way of getting into herding.

If you decide to enter competitions, you should study the official Herding Standard, laid down in 1990 by the Canadian Rottweiler Club, which is used as a blueprint by those in the Rottweiler herding community.

The Herding Standard

Some of the main points from the Standard are:
- The Rottweiler barks when necessary and, when he is working cattle, uses a very intimidating charge. Less force should be used when working sheep.
- The Rottweiler, when working cattle, will search out the dominant animal and challenge it. Upon proving his control over that animal he will then settle back and concentrate on his work.
- If worked on the same stock for any length of time, the Rottweiler tends to develop a bond with the stock and will become quite affectionate with them as long as they do what he says.
- The Rottweiler shows a gathering/fetching style when working sheep, and generally learns directions fairly quickly. He drives sheep with ease.

The instinct to herd is still very much part of a Rottweiler's makeup. Photo courtesy: Becket Group.

Learning Herding Skills

Probably the best way to learn is to find a club. Contact your national kennel club and/or local breed clubs. They should be able to provide you with details about a herding club near you, or the name of someone who actively practices the sport.

Tips for Beginners

- Start young. Your Rottie will learn much more quickly if he is introduced to herding while his mind is still very receptive to new things.
- However, do not begin until the puppy is 12 to 18 months old (when his bones and joints will be stronger), or he may become injured.
- If you introduce an adult dog to herding, it is usually much easier to achieve results with a female than a male dog.

- Always give lots of verbal praise and encouragement when your Rottweiler is behaving as required.
- Start off by herding ducks. Once your Rottie has mastered this, you can graduate to more challenging animals, such as sheep, and then cattle.
- Your Rottie's natural herding instincts mean that little formal training will be required. However, it is worth teaching him the commands for left and right, as with Obedience or Agility (see pages 69 and 75).
- Your Rottweiler should be easily controlled by you at all times when working with livestock. Before starting to train him for herding, you should make sure that your Rottie's obedience is second to none. The *down* and *stay* control commands are particularly useful. To review these commands, see Chapter Two.

RIGHT-HAND DOG

Tracy St. Clair-Pearce keeps several varieties of rare Shetland breeds, including cattle, sheep, ducks, and geese. Thirteen-year-old Rottie female, Helga, has been working as Tracy's assistant for 12 years, earning her keep as a herding dog.

"I found I needed a right arm when it came to lambing and calving, and Helga, who accompanies me everywhere, just turned out to be naturally good at herding. I didn't have to give her very much in the way of training—she was a natural. We learned to put commands to actions.

"The animals can get a bit feisty and attack the dog, so I taught Helga how to ask permission to shake the animal off and get them back in line. She was extremely patient with them. She always asked permission to

retaliate, and I have never witnessed an animal being hurt by Helga. In fact, she is the one at risk since my cattle and sheep are a primitive breed with horns and the ability to use them! Helga really is the gentlest of souls, and since the age of two has been a Therapy dog.

"As a working dog, Helga has proved her worth to me time and time again. I had never taught Helga how to back up a cow (walk backwards), but she did it when I needed her to! I had a large, beef heifer who managed to escape through a hole in the fence into a field containing my rare Shetland bull.

"We had no idea how we were going to separate the heifer and the bull. Helga had a plan, though. She got between the two of them and literally forced the heifer to

Tracy St. Clair-Pearce working with Helga. Photo courtesy: Kentish Express.

back up across the entire field: right back to the gate, where the men were waiting to capture her. It was absolutely amazing. The other farmer said to me, 'Well, if I hadn't seen it with my own eyes I'd never have believed it!' Helga then removed the whole herd of beef heifers to another field so that it didn't happen again.

"One event, which really shows off Helga's gentler side, happened when I kept Bronze turkeys. When I used to move the moms and chicks around the yard, Helga would help. She would pick up any stragglers in her mouth and carry them to the new location. Then she'd gently spit them out. It was quite funny to see this chick, completely unharmed but extremely soggy, trying to shake off the drool and rearrange its ruffled feathers.

"Helga also saved the life of one of my valuable ewe lambs. I don't know how it happened, but the lamb had become separated from the rest of the flock and got lost. I had taken Helga out before to gather up stray members of the flock, so I thought I'd try to find the ewe with her.

"We went down the valley adjacent to the field. Helga seemed to know exactly where she was going. She went in as straight a line as possible, including right through two fences! Thinking that Helga thought she was on a walk, and seeing no sign of the ewe in the big, flat field we had just come to, I was getting close to the point of giving up and going home. But Helga just looked at me as if to say, 'Come on Mom, not too much further. It's this way.' So we went over and found the ewe stuck down a ditch in the field—which was why we did not see her.

"The ditch was covered over with a dilapidated old fence, which the ewe had fallen through and had gotten trapped. Her foreleg, which was really badly swollen, was caught in the fence and she was suspended by it. She made a full recovery, but if Helga and I hadn't found her she would have almost certainly lost her leg, and possibly even her life.

"I think it's fair to say that Helga is completely invaluable to me, and I owe her a lot."

TRACKING AND WORKING TRIALS

Tracking requires the dog to follow a human scent trail on the ground. Rottweilers have a superb sense of smell, which can easily be honed for tracking purposes.

There are significant differences between Tracking in the U.S. and in the U.K. In the United Kingdom, Tracking features in Working Trials; in the United States, it is a recreational pursuit all on its own.

British Working Trials

Working Trials involve Tracking, Agility, and Obedience, and test the dog's accuracy, concentration, temperament, and strength.

The Working Trials Stakes are progressively more difficult. For example, the Companion Dog (CD) Stake involves

- *Heeling* on and off a leash
- *Recall*
- *Sendaway*

Agility is one of the elements tested in Working Trials.

- Two-minute *sit*
- 10-minute *down*
- Clear jump
- Long jump
- *Scale, stay, recall*
- Retrieving a dumbbell
- Elementary search

The ultimate test in Working Trials is the Stake of Patrol Dog. This tests the dog's advanced control, agility, and nosework, as well as including a category on searching for criminals:

- Quartering the ground
- Test of courage
- Search and escort
- *Recall* from criminal
- Pursuit and detention of criminal

To achieve such a high level of control, you must attend a Working Trials club for special training.

American Tracking

There is no Working Trials equivalent in the United States. Many of the elements seen in Working Trials are tested in Obedience and Agility. Consequently, Tracking is a sport in its own right.

American Tracking has three titles.

- **Tracking Dog (TD):** A dog must follow a recent track (laid thirty minutes to two hours previously). The track of 440–500 yards (0.40–0.45 km) will involve between three and five changes of direction. The dog is also expected to retrieve or indicate the location of an article (e.g., a glove or wallet).
- **Tracking Dog Excellent (TDX):** A dog must follow an older track (laid three to five hours previously). The track is longer (800–1000 yards/0.73–0.91 km), more turns are involved, and more demanding physical and scenting obstacles have to be

Give your Rottie a strong, positive command at the start of the track.

Continue to give encouragement as the scent is followed.

overcome (such as crosstracks). The dog should retrieve or indicate four different articles, all approximately the same size.

• **Variable Surface Tracking (VST):** This is the urban equivalent of the more traditional

tracking titles, which are based in countryside surroundings. The track is 600–800 yards (0.55–0.73 km) long, laid three to five hours previously, and may take the dog down a street or through a building. The dog's ability to track on different surfaces is also tested (vegetation, concrete, asphalt, gravel, sand, etc.).

Teaching Tracking

If you decide to learn how to track with your Rottie, you should, ideally, do so through a training club. A club will teach you how to track properly, without picking up any bad habits along the way, as well as showing you the correct harness to purchase and use. However, the following exercise can be used as a "taster" to see if tracking may be the next great hobby for you and your dog. It is a good idea to try this exercise with the help of a friend.

• Find a field of grass. The grass should, ideally, be no more than 18 inches (46 cm) high.
• You will need a tracking pole. To begin with, you can use an ordinary garden cane. Your Rottie will come to associate the pole as the starting point of the trail. The dog needs to be focused.
• You should also use a tracking harness. Putting on the tracking harness acts as a signal to the dog, informing him that a trail has started and he needs to be focused on the job at hand. It is also safer, as the harness distributes tension evenly over the dog's shoulders, rather than concentrating on the throat.

- Get a friend to hold your dog at the tracking pole.
- Walk forward about 65 feet/21 yards (20 m), sliding your feet along the grass as you do so. The purpose of this is to crush the grass, making a scent for the dog to follow.
- At the end of your trail, stop. Make sure you have your dog's attention, and drop one of his favorite toys on the ground.
- Do an about-turn and walk back to the tracking pole.
- Taking your Rottie from your friend, and making sure your dog is facing the right direction, ask him to *"Track."*
- Encourage him to move forward on the *track* command. He should soon pick up the trail.
- Do not forget to reward him handsomely when he successfully follows the track and retrieves the toy you dropped.
- Once he starts to improve, drop his toy about halfway along the trail. This will encourage him to put his nose to the ground to smell the trail. This is important for when you start to incorporate changes of direction (see right).
- Repeat the above exercise on different types of ground.
- Always remember that sessions are best kept short and fun. Don't overdo things or your Rottie will become bored and frustrated.

Once your Rottweiler has mastered this basic maneuver, you can gradually increase the length of the trail and its difficulty.

- Increase the length of the track to about 130 feet/45 yards (40 m).
- Ask your Rottie to track a longer trail like this four or five times.
- Once he is confident, lay a trail *without* sliding your feet along the ground (make sure your footsteps are not so far apart that your dog loses the trail).
- Gradually increase the length of the trail to about 300 feet/100 yards (90 m).

Now introduce changes in direction.
- Trample the grass at the point where you want the trail to make a sharp change in direction. This makes the change more obvious to your Rottie's nose. Over time, he will pick up changes in direction from more subtle clues.
- Extend the trail from the point of the turn, at a 90-degree angle.
- About 10 feet (3 m) along the new direction, drop a toy.
- Your Rottie will make it clear when he has found the new toy. Praise him and then ask him to continue tracking. This will teach him that he has been successful, but that it is not over yet. He will remain alert to other changes in direction.
- Gradually increase the time between when the trail is laid and when your Rottie tries to pick it up.
- Always reward your dog after every session so that he remains eager to track.

FOLLOW THAT SCENT!

Barbara Butler has bred Rottweilers for more than 30 years, during which time she has bred numerous tracking dogs. Now 84 years old, Barbara recounts some of her experiences:

"Rottweilers make excellent tracking dogs, because their sense of smell is superb—they have one of the best noses in the business.

"Smell is only one small part of the makeup of a good tracking dog, though. One of the most important features is an excellent temperament. Tracking dogs need to be intelligent, outgoing, totally fearless, energetic, steady, and responsive. Rottweilers more than fit the mold. They have a working heritage and are happiest when doing something active.

"I entered my first Working Trial competition with a lovely Rottie called Gallant Crusader. There weren't that many training classes around at the time, so we ended up having to learn everything from a book! We didn't seem to suffer for it too much, though, because in our first competition, we got a certificate of merit at CD Stake.

Ch. Upend Gallant Theoderic, one of Barbara's best tracking dogs.

"If you're going to train a Rottie, you need to be consistent, positive, and kind. You won't get too far training a dog by making him scared of punishment. He'll just resent you for it and become uncooperative.

"I learned the value of positive thinking in a Working Trials Stake I entered. On the course, there was a 6-foot scale jump that I knew Gallant Crusader could not do. It was worrying me quite a lot, and I mentioned this in passing to another competitor. She turned around and said, 'Well, he won't then, will he?'

"I asked her what she meant and she responded, 'If you don't believe in your dog, he won't believe in you. He'll sense your misgivings about the jump and it will worry him into not achieving it.' She was right of course—we missed the jump. I learned from that, and from then on I've tried to approach everything with a positive attitude.

"It is amazing what tracking dogs can achieve. I used to train with a club every Sunday. We'd stop at lunchtime and go for a meal. Just before leaving for lunch we would lay a trail for the more advanced dogs. By the time we came back after lunch the trail would be an hour or two old, so it posed more of a challenge for the dogs.

"One day, we came out after lunch and it had been snowing. The trail we had laid for the dogs was covered by an inch and a half of snow. I never expected the dogs to follow that trail, but they did—with no difficulty. It just goes to show that our canine friends are probably a great deal more intelligent and capable than most people think."

CARTING

Carting, in which a dog is harnessed to a small cart, is not a recognized sport in the U.K. or the U.S. To date, the only country in which carting is an official canine sport is South Africa. In Britain and the U.S. today, carting is seen mostly at parades and demonstrations. The sport can be an extremely good method of entertainment. Children, in particular, love wheeling around in a Rottie-drawn cart.

If carting appeals to you, do not rush straight out and buy a cart. The wrong type of cart, improperly harnessed and loaded, could cause a great deal of damage to your Rottie. It is vital to secure the help of someone who knows what they are doing. Contact your national kennel club or Rottweiler breed association for details, or try to find a local enthusiast.

SHOWING YOUR ROTTWEILER

Exhibiting your Rottweiler can be great fun. You will get to know lots of like-minded people,

meet a lot of other Rottweilers, and, hopefully, win a few competitions.

Showing is not all about bright lights and fame, however. It is hard work! The cost of traveling all over the country with your dog and equipment in tow is considerable. Competition is fierce, and to achieve any sort of success you will have to spend a lot of time making sure that your Rottie is in peak condition.

To Show or Not to Show

In most countries only registered animals are allowed to take part on the show circuit, so find out whether your Rottie is listed with your national kennel club.

The second is to obtain a copy of the Breed Standard and see how your Rottweiler measures up. Breed Standards vary between countries. Your national kennel club will be able to provide a copy of the full Standard (a summary appears in Chapter Seven).

Carting is a popular sight at parades, fairs, and demonstrations.

It takes a lot of hard work to build a successful partnership in the show ring.

Meeting the Standards

Once they have decided to show, many people choose a new puppy they hope has the potential to succeed all the way to the top. Most breeders will be happy to help you choose a puppy with good show potential—after all, any success will reflect favorably on their kennels. However, be warned: There is no guarantee that the promising little puppy will be good enough to win anything, and the breeder cannot be held responsible if that turns out to be the case—they are not fortune-tellers! Should this happen, you must be prepared to keep your Rottweiler puppy as a much-loved pet.

Ring Training

You need to make sure that your Rottie makes the most of himself and that he learns to enjoy the show experience. The best way to achieve this is to join a ring training class. Your Rottie will be taught how to stand and move correctly. Classes will also improve your abilities as a handler.

BECOMING A CHAMPION

The criteria for becoming a Champion differs between the U.S. and the U.K. In Britain, a dog that achieves three Challenge Certificates ("tickets") under three different judges in three separate shows becomes a Champion.

In the U.S., competition is based on a points system. American Rottweilers have to achieve 15 points in licensed ("championship") shows to become a Champion. The maximum number of points an animal can win at a show is five, so a would-be Champion must win points in at least three shows, under three different judges. Of the 15 points required, two must be "majors" (scores of three, four, or five points).

Standing

Standing still in the show ring is your Rottie's opportunity to show the judge how good a specimen of the breed he is; his posture should display his body to maximum advantage. In Britain, dogs are trained to acquire this position naturally, known as free standing. In the U.S., Rotties are "stacked." "Stacking" a dog requires the handler to pick up each foot and manually place it on the floor. The back legs are slightly outstretched behind, while the front legs should be straight (angled neither forward nor backward). After placing the legs, the handler holds the dog's collar, encouraging him to look forward and to extend his neck. The aim of stacking is to distribute more evenly the dog's weight, thus lengthening his spine, which shows the Rottie to maximum advantage.

When your Rottie is standing still in the ring, the judge will take the opportunity to examine him closely. He or she will check dentition, coat quality, and conformation. How your dog behaves during this examination is important, as his temperament will be under scrutiny as well.

Gait/Movement

Your dog's movement will also be assessed by the judge. The different national Breed Standards all describe the Rottweiler's gait as balanced, positive, and harmonious, conveying an impression of "trotting." Your Rottie will be assessed against this Standard as he moves around the ring.

Conformation is assessed when the dog is standing four-square in a show pose.

Top Tips

Showing is great fun, but it pays to keep your feet (or paws!) on the ground. Always remember

- Your Rottie is special. He should be treated as a pet first and foremost, and only then as a show dog.
- Start off by going to shows as a spectator. Get to know the dogs, and talk to the breeders. You'll be surprised what you can pick up!

- Join a breed club, and attend its seminars.
- Go to ring training classes. Remember that if you are going to achieve success with a dog, *you* must not let *him* down with incorrect handling.
- Make sure you look just as well groomed as your Rottie.
- Do not become disheartened. It takes a lot of time, money, patience, and hard work to achieve success.

GET THE SHOW ON THE ROAD

Jo Prouse's interest in the show world started with a German Shepherd that she exhibited at fun exemption shows. Her interest escalated when she acquired her first Rott, Fantasa Sapphire n' Steel (Ben).

"We started off by going to classes, and then entered a few shows. Talk about fun and games! Ben constantly had his nose to the floor, and he wanted to sit at every opportunity.

"The experience didn't put me off, though. We entered a few more shows and did very well. Ben was consistently placed, and it gave me confidence to enter a Championship show.

"I spent the whole of the day before the show bathing and grooming Ben and had to get up at 4 A.M. to drive to the show. By the time I got into the ring I felt exhausted, sick, and had a headache from worrying.

"I was awarded my fourth position in a haze. It was only afterwards I realized that, for a beginner, fourth is actually extremely good.

"We continued to do well. Ben went on to win Best Puppy, beating hundreds of other puppies in the process. By now, I was enjoying the show world so much that I decided to get a female Rottie, Fantasa Navy Wren (Sophie).

Jo Prouse with Sophie, a late developer that has blossomed in the ring. Photo: David Dalton.

"Sophie took quite a while to mature properly, and our winning patterns were a bit erratic. Sometimes we'd do really well for a couple of months and then we wouldn't win a thing for the next six. I was beginning to become very disheartened and at one stage I considered giving up.

"Just when I was getting to the point of quitting, Sophie came first in her class, and we had to go up against all the other bitch winners for the Challenge Certificate.

"I didn't think we stood a chance, but then I suddenly found myself being called forward by the judge so that Fantasa Navy Wren could receive her CC. I was on top of the world and completely speechless!

"Not too much later, Sophie won another CC, her second. She also won Best of Breed as well as gaining a Reserve CC. Now Sophie's success gives me the best-ever feeling, especially since her wins mean she is eligible to enter Crufts every year. It's amazing, really. At one time, I used to go to this fantastic show to watch—never thinking that, one day, I would be showing a dog of my own there!

"Right now, Sophie and I are trying to gain that third CC, which will make her a Champion. Never, in my wildest dreams, did I think we would achieve this!"

CHAPTER SIX

A SPECIAL BOND

Because he was originally bred as a working dog, the Rottweiler likes to be kept occupied. The breed has lost none of its working ability, and the Rottweiler's diligent, eager attitude has been put to good use by various organizations.

His natural instincts to guard and to protect are an asset to police forces, but the breed's gentleness and great love of people also means that the Rottie is found in other "careers," such as therapy dog work and as an assistance (service) dog, as the following case histories show.

POLICE DOG

When you think of police dogs, you are likely to conjure up the image of a German Shepherd Dog. However, it was actually as a police dog that the Rottweiler came to be as popular as he is today.

As we have seen in Chapter One, the introduction of railroad networks toward the end of the 19th century meant the breed was no longer needed to drive cattle over long distances. Rottweilers looked likely to die out in Germany, but they were taken on as police dogs.

From there they went from strength to strength, attracting the attention of the general public, and eventually becoming a popular pet the world over.

Although the German Shepherd Dog still dominates the world of police dogs, the Rottie hasn't forgotten his instincts and still has a lot to offer the police services.

His natural guarding and protecting instincts, his courage and versatility, his great intelligence, keen nose, and aptitude for learning all hold him in good stead for police and army work. Plus he's a loving, loyal companion off duty, as Sergeant Gary Dace (see case history overleaf) will testify.

BEN THERE, DONE THAT!

Sergeant Gary Dace is one of the few police dog handlers who works a Rottweiler. When he first started training Ben, three years ago, there were just seven other Rottweilers in service in the U.K. Numbers have grown slightly since then, but, compared to the ubiquitous German Shepherd Dog, the Rottie is very much in the minority.

"My first police dog, Max, was a Shepherd," says Gary. "We did very well, and went to the National Trials together. When Max retired, I was given another Shepherd, but it didn't work out—he was too nervous. Luckily for me, a Rottweiler had been given back to a breeder that we dealt with. There had been a death in the family, and the owners were no longer able to look after him, so we took him on.

"The Rottweiler brings the same qualities to the job as does the German Shepherd—tracking, searching, etc. The only problem is that many of the public think Rottweilers are dangerous. We attended a mini-riot recently. Because Ben bit someone, there was a huge outcry over how the police use dangerous dogs. The German Shepherds had bitten too, but no one was concerned about that. Ben is not dangerous, but when he is required to work, whether that is to search or to apprehend, he does his job, just like any other police dog.

"Ben has a great memory. With some dogs, if you don't train something for a few months, they start to forget it. Not with Ben. He retains everything.

Police dog Ben shows all that is best in the Rottweiler temperament.

"We've tried six other Rotties at this training unit, but they didn't work out; they were too soft. Ben is soft when he's not working. He lives at home with me; my 12-year-old daughter and Ben are best friends. He's a very affectionate dog, very loving and loyal. He can also be incredibly stubborn and arrogant though. You can never *make* a Rottweiler work—he has to *want* to work for you. Luckily, he enjoys all aspects of his job, so there are usually few problems.

"Ben has had great success at work. He was awarded a certificate of merit for bravery for his actions when a female with a handgun started shooting at me and at other police officers. It was actually a gas-charged air pistol, but we were told it was a revolver and that she had two rounds. Ben took her down and disarmed her without hesitation.

"Ben has tracked down offenders from stolen motor vehicles, burglars, people the police had lost, stolen property, and even an escaped prisoner. He really is a tremendous working dog.

"When we are out and about, people in my area see how good-natured he is, and he has an excellent reputation. It's important for people to see the other side of the breed—the soft side. Ben and I do public displays at shows, where one minute he'll be disarming someone with a gun, and the next he'll be in the crowd, being patted by all the children. This shows the two sides of him—the soft, lovely natured dog, and the eager, hard worker.

A true partnership: Ben with Sergeant Gary Dace.

"Ben is not just a dog (in his opinion, too!) or a tool of my trade, but my partner and constant companion. Above all, he is a treasured member of our family and loved by all."

DOG FOR THE DISABLED

Assistance dogs help a variety of people— from the blind or the deaf to people who are unable to walk or who have limited mobility. Although a number of breeds are used as assistance dogs—from Papillons to German Shepherds—the Rottweiler is rarely, if ever, called upon.

Because he is such a large breed, the Rottie can be difficult to handle for someone who may be frail. Being an intelligent, naturally dominant dog, the Rottie needs a handler with dog experience and with the right personality to command the dog's respect.

The public's negative perception of the breed plays a big part too. The burden of responsibility placed upon a Rottie assistance dog's shoulders is a heavy one. One perceived wrong move, and the press will have a field day.

However, this is not to say that Rotties are necessarily unsuitable for this kind of work, as the following case history shows.

ONE IN A MILLION

When dog behaviorist Sue Lee took on a rescue Rottie nine years ago, she had no idea how much she would grow to rely on him, and how much he would change her life.

"Ninja was just a few months old when I got him. He was a very dominant pup, and was quite naughty. He'd dig up all the bushes in the garden and drag them into the kitchen. One night, when I went out to get the wash in from the backyard, I fell down a three-foot hole that hadn't been there before! All Ninja really needed, though, was training, and basic rules.

"When I first had him, I was a security officer, and he would work with me. He didn't have a vicious streak in him, though, and I had to teach him to bark on command. Seeing him bark was enough to ward off most people.

"When I became a dog behaviorist, Ninja continued to work with me. He was so good with other dogs—rock solid—and so I could trust him with the problem cases I took on. With those that were aggressive to other dogs, I used Ninja to help rehabilitate them. Whatever the other dog was doing, Ninja would just sit there, totally unfazed by it. He was so totally laid back, it taught aggressive dogs to stop seeing him as a threat, and to ignore him.

"One time, I had a problem dog staying at my house. I took him out one day to go to a good walking place, but he tried to jump out of the car. I twisted around to grab him, but he was pulling away, and I felt a 'ping' in my back. I couldn't feel anything on my left side. I had damaged three discs in my lower back, and a couple in my neck. I ended up in a wheelchair, and was incapable of doing anything for six months. Because I lived

Ninja: A remarkable Rottweiler.

alone, I had to have friends come and look after me and walk Ninja.

"But I was determined to walk Ninja myself, so I would take a walker out, with Ninja tethered to it. He'd take one small step, then stop and look at me, to check that I was okay. He never pulled.

"I progressed to crutches—and I will always have to use them. I can't bend and so am unable to pick up anything I drop. Although Rottweilers aren't natural retrievers, I decided to teach Ninja to fetch items for me. First, I taught him to hold something, and then he went on to pick up dropped articles and bring them to me naturally. We had a few laughs, though, as Ninja wasn't able to distinguish which shoe matched another to make a pair, so we'd sit there while he brought piles of boots and shoes. I thanked him for each one, until I ended up with a matching pair!

"To teach Ninja to empty the washing machine, I placed a piece of cheese in the back of it to get him used to putting his head in the machine. He loved cheese, so he would dive in to get it. Then I'd put the cheese behind a sock, and he'd bring the sock to me, then go back in and get his cheese reward. Gradually, more wash was put in, and less cheese.

"Although Ninja could do so much for me in the home, I wanted him to be officially recognized, so he could be allowed everywhere with me—shops, restaurants, etc. I contacted the charity Dogs for the Disabled, which doesn't usually register dogs people have trained themselves, but they do consider exceptional cases. When I said the dog was a Rottweiler, the phone went dead for a while, but they came around to assess him.

"Dogs for the Disabled had to be convinced that Ninja could be relied on. With the press image of the Rottweiler, it was vital that he was rock solid because he would

Ninja helped to rectify the public stereotype of Rottweilers.

be representing the charity when he was wearing his jacket. The assessments included us walking through busy shopping areas, with security guards wearing helmets coming over to pat him on the head, etc. In one shopping center, there was a little Jack Russell that was going mad at Ninja, barking and trying to aggravate him. Ninja just put his head down and walked straight past him.

"When Ninja qualified, he had to have a special coat made, as they didn't have one large enough for him—they all looked like pimples on elephants! Ninja had never worn a jacket before, and I thought he'd do his best to get it off, but the first time it was put on, he walked around as if he was as proud as punch.

"I started doing fund-raising talks for the charity, and everyone we met made a great fuss of Ninja. Whenever he wore his jacket, people would approach us and say they'd never seen a Rottie doing this job before. When he wasn't wearing his jacket, it seemed people would rather jump in front of a bus than walk past Ninja!

"The only things that unnerved Ninja were hedgehogs! We had a family of them in the backyard and he was terrified of them. At night, he'd go to the kitchen door and peep out to see if they were there. If they were, he'd refuse to go out, and would rather burst than go out on his own. He was only brave enough if I went with him!

"He was always gentle with other animals. One time, he was restless all day, and kept running to a little table I had in the hall. There was nothing on it, and I told him there was nothing there, but all day he kept running back and forth. In the end, exasperated, I went to the table and moved it—only to find a little sparrow was hiding underneath it! Ninja looked very smug, as if to say 'I told you there was something there!'

"Ninja was retired about a year ago. He had developed arthritis and it wasn't fair to make him continue to work, so I got a replacement Dog for the Disabled—Sweep, a Labrador. Although he was used to sharing his home with other dogs, I was worried about how Ninja would react to having another dog doing things for me. Actually, he seemed really relieved that another dog could do all the hard work for a change!

"He would supervise Sweep to make sure he was doing the job right, but wouldn't interfere. He even let Sweep get the wash out, which was one of his favorite tasks. There was one job he wouldn't let Sweepie do, though. The moment I called 'Shoes,' he'd run after Sweep and nudge him out of the way so that he could fetch the shoes himself. Apparently, it's usual for a retired dog to want to keep one little job as their own.

"Ninja's condition worsened. He had a ramp for the car, so he could get in and out, but he wouldn't use it. Sweep would race up and down it as if it were an Agility ramp, but Ninja wasn't interested. His coat started falling out, and he lost 9 pounds (4 kg) in two weeks. The veterinarian suspected Cushing's Disease and it was decided that it was fairer to put Ninja to sleep.

"Ninja had always been with me, so it was a hard blow. Even before I was disabled, he had always worked with me. Ninja was special—there'll never be another. They broke the mold when they made Ninja."

THERAPY DOG

You won't need telling how wonderful it is to have a dog—the cuddles, the unconditional love, the fun, smiles, and laughter. A loving dog can lift your spirits instantly. Imagine then how empty your life would be if you could no longer share your life with one. This is the situation that many people face—those who live in residential homes where there may be a "no dogs" policy, or those whose health means they are no longer able to look after a dog.

Thankfully, there are teams of volunteers who give their time to share their dogs with such people, visiting hospices, hospitals, residential homes, schools, and even prisons. The dogs are all character-assessed and must be completely trustworthy.

Interacting with a dog has scientifically proven benefits, lowering stress and blood pressure, relieving anxiety, and boosting the immune system. The most visible result of the visits, however, is the number of instantly smiling faces you see when you walk into a room with your dog. It's no wonder they call them therapy dogs!

FLOWER POWER

Valerie Crofts, a coordinator for Pets as Therapy (PAT), a charity that promotes a dog-visiting program, has two therapy dogs, and has had another in the past.

"Daisy is five years old and has been a therapy dog since she was 18 months old. I've started taking Iza along to some visits; at 19 months old, he is a trainee.

"I registered Daisy as a therapy dog as she has such a super temperament— she is loved by everybody. She doesn't have an aggressive bone in her body. I had a car accident years ago, and had relied on the help of many people to support me, so I thought it was about time that *I* started to help people.

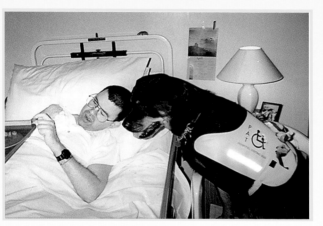

Daisy with her friend Peter.

"Daisy and Iza have been visiting a residential therapeutic project for abused and damaged children. The children are taken out, one by one, for a walk with Daisy and a teacher, and Daisy has fun playing fetch with them. Those that are left in the classroom interact with Iza, who plays dead when you say 'Bang,' which the children love!

"I also take Daisy to a home for the elderly. She is always perfectly behaved, but she has her favorite people and visits them without fail. They are usually the ones that save their cookies for her!

"One lady at the home had suffered multiple strokes, and would just sit in her chair all day. A nurse thought that she must have had dogs in the past, and so we took Daisy to meet her.

"There was no reaction at first, but the second time we went, she got really excited when she saw Daisy. She couldn't speak, but was making lots of noises. We took the lady's hand and put it on Daisy's head so she could feel her, and she clearly enjoyed it.

"Another lady we visited had also been seriously ill. The next time I saw her, she said that she had been given just three days to live, and that if it hadn't been for Daisy, she wouldn't still be around. This amazed me. I didn't think we really had that much of an effect. I thought we just went along and had a chat with people; I didn't realize how much we were giving to them.

"Peter is a particular favorite with Daisy. He has multiple sclerosis and diabetes, and is confined to his bed. Daisy has to climb on a chair to get to see him. I give Peter some treats to give to Daisy; if he gets the shakes, Daisy has to wait until Peter can control them before she gets her treat. I didn't realize how sensitive Peter's skin was until I once wiped off some slobber from his fingers. We have taught Daisy just to lick the treat gently from Peter's hand, so that she doesn't cause him any pain.

"There's such a stigma with Rottweilers, it's nice for people to see that the majority are good."

CHAPTER SEVEN

SEEKING PERFECTION

Every Rottweiler owner believes he or she has the most perfect, beautiful dog in the world, though only a small minority are considered worthy of winning in the show ring. So, what distinguishes a "good" example of a Rottie from an "average" example, or even a "poor" one? Answer: the degree to which it matches the ideal Rottie as laid out in the Breed Standard.

WHAT IS A BREED STANDARD?

When humans domesticated dogs, they were bred to help out in various functions—to hunt, to retrieve, to guard, to herd, to be companions, etc. Through trial and error, dogs were selectively bred for particular features that enabled them to do their particular "job." A beautiful, glamorous Maltese that excels at being a companion dog wouldn't last long herding sheep; likewise, a Border Collie would go crazy if he was expected to sit on someone's lap all day and be pampered.

A Rottie is built as he is in order to drive livestock. To make sure each breed retains its unique qualities, a Breed Standard is drawn up. This is a written blueprint of the ideal Rottie from head to tail. It is this Standard against which all dogs are judged, and to which all breeders should aspire.

BREED STANDARD: KEY POINTS

Ask your national kennel club for a copy of the Rottweiler Breed Standard for your country. The Standards vary only slightly, and the key points common to them all are given below.

General Appearance

A dog that was bred to manage cows needed to be large enough to be imposing while still being able to move and turn easily, so the ideal Rottweiler should be a robust, noble-looking dog of medium-large size. The dog should be compact but powerful, capable of great strength, endurance, and agility.

The Rottweiler is a dog of strength and substance.

Characteristics

Confidence, courage, and self-assurance are the breed's key characteristics, qualities necessary for the Rottie to control animals much larger than himself.

Temperament

Although he needed to be tenacious with the cattle, the Rottie had to work with his human handler too. For this reason, he needed to be good-natured and certainly not aggressive or shy. He has strong guarding instincts, relating to when he would need to guard his cattle against predators or thieves. He can be aloof with strangers.

Head and Skull

The medium-length head should be broad between the ears (to accommodate the dog's large brain). The forehead should be slightly arched, and although the skin should not be loose, a moderate wrinkle is acceptable when the dog is alert. The approximate ratio of the length of the muzzle compared to the distance from the stop (the indentation between the eyes) to the occiput (the top point at the back of the head) should be 2:3.

The black nose should be broad rather than round, with quite large nostrils. This is necessary for the dog to get the maximum amount of oxygen to his lungs when working.

Eyes

The medium-sized, dark, almond-shaped eyes should neither protrude nor recede.

Ears

The triangular ears are pendant, meaning they hang down. They are placed quite high on the skull and wide apart (so the dog is sensitive to sounds all around him). The ears fall forward, reaching to the middle of the dog's cheeks.

The head is broad and noble.

The legs are straight and muscular.

Mouth

The dog's dentition should be complete (20 upper teeth, 22 lower teeth), forming a scissor bite, where the upper teeth closely overlap the lower ones. The Rottie would need strong teeth to nip stubborn cattle into action. The flews (lips) should be firm—not loose or hanging—and should be black.

Neck

The slightly arched neck should be of moderate length, well muscled and strong. The skin should be well fitting—not loose or "throaty."

Forequarters

The shoulders are long, sloping, and well laid back. The legs are straight and muscular, with heavy, strong bone. The pasterns (between the dog's "wrist" and toes) are almost perpendicular to the ground, but slope slightly forward.

Body

The broad, deep chest with well-sprung ribs should allow plenty of heart and lung room for the working dog. The back should be straight and not too long (the back should be only slightly longer than the height of the dog to the shoulder). The loins (the narrowest point of the dog's "waist") should be short, strong, and well muscled.

Hindquarters

The upper and lower thighs should be muscular and strong. Because the Rottie would be expected to trot over long distances, he needs good shock absorbers. To achieve this, the stifles (the dog's "knees") should be well bent, and the hock joints (the "heels") should be well angulated and very strong. The rear pasterns should be almost perpendicular to the ground. When viewed from behind, the hindlegs should be straight and strong.

The hindquarters are muscular with well-angulated hocks.

Feet

Like everything else about the Rottweiler, the feet should be strong. A hard-working dog needs good "work boots." The feet should be round and compact, with thick, tough pads, arched toes, and short, dark nails (which tend to be stronger than pale nails). The hind feet should be slightly longer than the front feet, and the rear dewclaws should be removed.

Tail

The tail (which is customarily docked) should be carried level with the topline, giving the appearance that it is an extension of the dog's back. It can be carried slightly above this level when the dog is excited.

Gait/Movement

The Rottweiler is a trotter whose body is designed to cover as much ground as effortlessly and efficiently as possible. He should have great endurance and strength. When moving, the level of the back should remain motionless.

Coat

The Rottweiler's coat is designed to protect him from the elements. The top coat should be straight, flat, and coarse. The insulating undercoat (which shouldn't be seen through the top coat) is essential on the neck and thighs.

Color

The coat color is black, with clearly defined markings (rust/tan to mahogany) over each eye, on the cheeks, along each side of the muzzle, on

The Rottweiler must cover the ground effortlessly and efficiently.

the throat, as triangles on each side of the breastbone, on the forelegs, on the inside of the rear legs, and underneath the tail. The undercoat should be gray, tan/fawn, or black.

Size

The U.K. Kennel Club Standard suggests 25–27 inches (63–69 cm) for males, and 23–25 inches (58–63.5 cm) for females. The American Standard allows a slightly wider range, reducing the lower guide height by an inch—males can be 24–27 inches (60.5–69 cm) and females 22–25 inches (56–63.5 cm).

TYPES OF BREEDING

Some dogs are closer to perfection than others. There is no surefire way of producing the ideal Rottie.

There are three types of breeding available to a breeder—linebreeding, outcrossing, and inbreeding, but the latter is rarely used because of health implications that can sometimes result.

Linebreeding

This involves mating dogs that are related but are not close relatives; for example, dogs that share the same grandfather, rather than the incestuous mother-son, brother-sister, etc., matings of inbreeding.

Linebreeding is the type used by most breeders in the U.K. By mating dogs that look similar (because they are related), this type of breeding can help to "fix" a "type," passing on the best qualities of the line to the next generation.

Of course, genes are no connoisseurs of quality, and so the bad characteristics of the line can also be consolidated in an unwise mating, thus passing on, at best, cosmetic defects to the next generation and, at worse, serious health problems.

Ch. Fantasa Bronze Bruin, bred and handled by Liz Dunhill and owned by Fred and Sharon Baker.

Parents	Grandparents	Great-Grandparents	Great-Great-Grandparents
Ch. Pendley Winston	Pendley Jacob of Charledane	Ch. Caprido Minstrel of Potterspride	Ch. Chesara Dark Charles
			Lyric from Caprido
		Pendley Skylark	Ch. Chesara Dark Roisterer
			Ch. Nedraw Black Sunshine
	Pendley Gudrun	Pendley Leopold	Eiko v. d. Zigernerinsel at Herberger
			Pendley Skylark
		Ch. Pendley Jasmin	Ch. Caprido Minstrel of Potterspride
			Ch. Pendley Skylark
Ch. Fantasa Red Riding Hood	Ch. Poirot Wham	Chesara Dark Harry	Caprido Strolling Player from Chesara
			Ch. Chesara Dark Julia
		Poirot Jocana	Ch. Chesara Dark Charles
			Ch. Poirot Camilla
	Ch. Rottsann Regal Romance	Jagen Blue Andante	Ch. Janbicca The Superman
			Jagen Midnight Blue
		Rottsann Classic Crystal	Chesara Dark Herod
			Poirot Fantasia

Outcrossing

Outcrossing—where two completely unrelated dogs are mated together—is one of the safest types of breeding, as far as health is concerned (although the parents' lines should be checked beforehand). Genetically, it is good to introduce fresh blood—and fresh genes—to a line. With them come new qualities (and defects).

Outcrossing can be unpredictable. However, careful research into each dog's history and pedigree, and investigating the type of dogs they may have produced with other matings, can minimize the "wild card" factor.

Ch. Poirot Nazareth's father, Ponciana Atlas, was used because he has significant strengths to bring to the breed—strong character, good shoulders, size, and bone, a rich mahogany tan, and an impressive pedigree.

Outcross Ch. Poirot Nazareth, bred and owned by Ann Evans.

Parents	Grandparents	Great-Grandparents	Great-Great-Grandparents
Ponciana Atlas	Int. German Ch. Fürst v. Wolfert Turm	Gil v. Burgthann	Chris v. Obergrombacher Schloss
			Cora v. Ries
		Petra v. Fusse Der Eifel	Int. Ch. Falko v. d. Tente
			Hummel v. Fusse d. Eifel
	Mamba v. Bayern	Int. Ch. Doc v. Teufelsbrücke	Int. Ch. Benno v. d. Schwarzen Heide
			Ch. Bea v. d. Teufelsbrücke
		Dana v. d. Kolping Shöhe	Bulli v. Bayernland
			Conny v. Hegnenbacher Landl
Poirot Golden Earing	Poirot Cockney Rebel	Ch. Varenka The Secret Agent	Varenka The Senator
			Ch. Varenka Rare Secret
		Poirot Overture	Poirot The Ferryman
			Ch. Poirot Edwina
	Poirot Yana	Ch. Rottsann Golden Venture	Ch. Pendley Goldfinch
			Rottsann Classic Lines
		Poirot Uptown Girl	Ch. Upend Gallant Gairbert
			Poirot Jocana

PUPPY TO CHAMPION
Ch. Travillons Hattie

Ch. Travillons Hattie, owned and bred by Teresa and Trevor Killick, has to date three CCs and six Reserve CCs (winning one CC at Crufts).

Nine and a half weeks.

16 weeks.

Nine months.

Three years, and a Champion.

Just as there are many different ways of breeding a Champion, so there are different ways that puppies develop into one. Some Rottie pups look like stunning specimens of the breed at eight weeks and grow into heavenly adults; others may look like nothing special but blossom unexpectedly as they get older. The most disappointing ones are those that look so promising and lose their uniqueness as they mature. Along with good breeding, luck plays a big part in producing winners.

Pictured above is how one dog made the transition from puppy to Champion. Who knows? Maybe *your* Rottie pup will turn heads in the show ring when he grows up.

CHAPTER EIGHT

HEALTH CARE

**Trevor Turner
BVetMed, MRCVS**

R ottweilers have a long history as guarding, herding, and draft dogs. Bred for strength and courage, they are very active dogs that need plenty of exercise. With a height of 22–27 inches (56–69 cm) and a weight of 90–110 pounds (41–50 kg), they are formidable and intimidating if not controlled. However, they are naturally good-natured and courageous, without nervousness or aggression.

Rottweilers are popular on both sides of the Atlantic. In 1998, 75,000 Rottweilers were registered by the American Kennel Club and approximately 5,000 by the Kennel Club in Britain. In comparison, during that year, about the same number of German Shepherd Dogs were registered in the U.S. and 21,000 in Britain.

It is not surprising that, with such popularity, certain breed-specific problems are apparent. These involve various joint and bone disorders, including bone tumors, and also certain eye conditions. These are discussed separately later in the chapter.

PREVENTIVE CARE

One of the most important areas of preventive care involves correct and early training, together with proper nutrition and, of course, appropriate vaccination and parasite control.

Once you have acquired your puppy, call your veterinarian and discuss vaccinations, appointment policy, fees, etc. At the same time, find out whether the practice organizes puppy classes. Obviously, the sooner you can get your new Rottweiler puppy to meet other dogs, the better.

Training

On both sides of the Atlantic, Rottweilers have, in recent years, attracted an aggressive image. Aggression should never be tolerated and can largely be avoided with correct training. This should commence at the time of acquisition. As soon as you decide on a Rottweiler puppy, make inquiries regarding local training classes.

Many clubs will accept fully vaccinated puppies from four months of age on, but contact with your veterinarian will often lead to an introduction to puppy classes, which are invaluable for the socialization and training of your newly acquired Rottweiler and can commence even earlier.

For more information on training, see Chapter Two.

Vaccinations

Vaccination and inoculation are, for our purposes, synonymous. By definition, **vaccination** involves subjecting the body to a suspension of microorganisms that will stimulate immunity but not cause disease. To achieve this, the microorganisms have to be altered. They are either killed (inactivated) or weakened (attenuated).

Inoculation involves introducing the agent into the tissues of the body, usually by injection. Vaccination can involve other methods of introduction, e.g., by the administration of nasal drops, which is the routine method by which

vaccination against infectious tracheitis (kennel cough) is carried out.

The puppy acquires his first immunity from the mother while in the womb. The necessary antibodies cross the placenta from the mother to the puppy's bloodstream. As these antibodies wane, immunity is topped up by antibodies secreted in the milk. This is called **passive immunity** and, once the puppy is weaned, it soon fades.

Primary vaccination should be carried out as soon as the passive immunity has declined sufficiently to allow the puppy to respond to the vaccine. Some vaccines will stimulate the puppy to build up a solid, active immunity even in the face of circulating maternal antibodies. Their full vaccination can be completed by 10–12 weeks of age. This is an important step forward, particularly for the Rottweiler, since it allows socialization and training to commence that much earlier, without the puppy being vulnerable to potential killer diseases.

Initial immunity is acquired from the mother.

Booster Vaccinations

Vaccination does not last indefinitely and boosting will be required. Booster vaccinations have recently become a matter of concern for both veterinarians and dog owners. Canine vaccination, including boosting, involves the use of **polyvalent** (multivalent) vaccines that give protection against several diseases.

There is evidence that, in certain cases, their use can result in reactions, and the need for annual boosting has been questioned. However, it is my opinion that, with the Rottweiler, which has a higher than normal reported susceptibility to parvovirus disease, it is sensible to balance the risk against the advantages. Here, the risk of a reaction is considerably less than the possibility of contracting the disease if immunity fails.

It is important that veterinarians follow the manufacturers' instructions with any drugs, including vaccines. In order to obtain a product license, vaccine manufacturers have to submit evidence regarding the safety and efficacy of the product. With a vaccine, this includes the duration of immunity. At present, revaccination is under review by manufacturers. Some are suggesting that, with certain diseases, e.g., distemper and hepatitis, annual boosting may not be strictly necessary.

During more than 40 years' experience of canine practice, I have never had to treat a dog with a serious vaccine reaction, and, therefore, I would err on the side of safety, particularly in this breed, and choose overprotection rather than underprotection.

However, if you have any concerns, queries, or questions, discuss these carefully with your veterinarian at the time of primary vaccination. Veterinarians are only too ready today to acknowledge that the perfect vaccine has not yet been invented and will be prepared to discuss the risks and benefits for your particular animal in relation to disease prevalence in your locality.

Can We Measure Immunity?

Blood tests are available for both puppies and adult dogs that indicate the animal's level of immunity for any of the diseases covered by vaccination. These will give a guide to the necessity for revaccination. However, be forewarned: It is likely that the cost of testing for each disease will be as much as a combined booster against all the diseases. Cost apart, it is also arguable whether such testing is in the dog's best interest. Taking a blood sample from most puppies is a stressful procedure, as it is for a fair number of adult dogs. It is considerably more stressful than a booster vaccination that can cover anything up to six diseases with one simple, hardly felt injection.

Depending on the disease, some vaccines do not offer long-lasting immunity. The intranasal Bordetella bronchiseptica vaccine against infectious tracheitis/bronchitis—**kennel cough**—lasts only approximately eight months, which is about the same time as natural immunity after a bout of the condition. If not challenged by contact with the disease, immunity is likely to drop to dangerous levels in about six months. Therefore, if you are involved

If your Rottweiler regularly comes into contact with other dogs, it is important to vaccinate against kennel cough.

in a training program with your dog, or are regularly attending obedience classes, shows, etc., or even if you regularly board your dog, revaccination against Bordetella (kennel cough) every six months is money well spent.

This disease is described as having low mortality and high morbidity; it does not usually prove fatal, but the dog will often have an irritating cough for several weeks. Even when apparently recovered, the dog can still act as a carrier. Such a situation could be disruptive to any planned training program involving your new Rottweiler.

To further complicate matters, kennel cough is not caused by Bordetella alone. Parainfluenza virus is another contributor, and indeed in North America this virus is considered to be the major cause, whereas in Britain and the rest of Europe Bordetella (a bacterium) is considered to be the most important agent, with parainfluenza playing a secondary role. In addition, adenovirus and distemper virus also

play a part. These, and parainfluenza, are, of course, incorporated into the usual polyvalent (multivalent) vaccines that are administered.

Recently a new intranasal kennel cough vaccine has become available that not only contains Bordetella but also a parainfluenza component as well. This vaccine will reinforce immunity conferred by the conventional parainfluenza component incorporated into the normal inoculation.

Leptospira vaccines are also usually included in the primary vaccination course. These cover two serious bacterial diseases caused by Leptospira bacterial organisms, *L. canicola* and *L. icterohaemorrhagaie*. These are killed vaccines and provide protection for only about 12 months. Modified live virus vaccines, e.g., distemper or parvovirus, give a much longer period of protection, but this varies with the individual and the disease.

Nevertheless, with any multivalent vaccine, the manufacturer will advise readministration in relation to the immunity conferred by the shortest acting component.

Core and Noncore Vaccines

Acknowledging the drawbacks associated with some vaccines, there has been a move in the United States to divide vaccination into two groups: core vaccines and noncore vaccines.

Core vaccines protect against diseases that are serious, fatal, or difficult to treat. In the U.K., this includes distemper, parvovirus, and adenovirus (hepatitis). In the U.S., rabies is also included in this category of necessary protection.

As a result of the change in the quarantine laws in Great Britain, rabies vaccine is now freely available from veterinary surgeons and may well become a core vaccine in the not-too-distant future.

Noncore vaccines include Bordetella, Leptospirosis, Coronavirus, and Borrelia (Lyme disease). This latter vaccine, used widely in North America, is known to cause reactions in a number of dogs. Lyme disease is a tick-borne disease that is of considerable concern in North America. It does occur to a lesser extent in the U.K., where there is no currently licensed vaccine available.

Canine Distemper

Distemper is relatively rare in the U.K., solely due to vaccination. Signs (symptoms) include fever, diarrhea, and coughing with discharges from the nose and eyes. Sometimes the pads will harden, a sign of the so-called "hardpad" variant. Further signs—seizures, chorea (twitching of groups of muscles) and paralysis—can be seen in a high proportion of infected dogs. As mentioned, the distemper virus can be involved in the kennel cough syndrome.

Hepatitis

This is also known as adenovirus disease, and can show signs ranging from sudden death (peracute infection) to mild cases where the patient is just a bit "off color." Most cases begin with a fever, enlargement of all the lymph nodes (glands), and a swollen liver. During recovery "blue eye" can occur. This is due

to edema (swelling) of the cornea in front of the eye and the dog may look blind. Initially very troubling, this usually resolves quickly without impairing sight. Adenovirus can also be one of the components in the kennel cough syndrome.

Rabies

Rabies is present on all continents except Australia and Antarctica. Several countries, including the U.K., are free of the disease. This usually is due to geographical barriers; for example, the United Kingdom is surrounded by water. The virus does not survive long outside the body.

The vectors of the disease are wildlife, particularly foxes and bats, or stray dogs. Transmission is mainly by biting and the signs are due to disruption of the central nervous system by the virus. This is an extremely serious disease, communicable to humans (zoonotic disease). Vaccination using an inactivated (killed) vaccine is mandatory in many countries, including the United States.

With the change of quarantine regulations in Britain, rabies vaccines are now available from the veterinarian and are mandatory if you wish to travel to Europe and return with your Rottweiler under the PETS travel scheme.

Infectious Tracheitis/Bronchitis

This can be serious, particularly in very young and very old dogs. It causes a persistent cough and, as explained, in the United States parainfluenza virus is considered the main cause.

Older dogs are more at risk from infectious tracheitis.

A parainfluenza component is incorporated in most multivalent vaccines available on both sides of the Atlantic. Bordetellosis prevention is by separate intranasal vaccination. Recently, a combined parainfluenza/Bordetella vaccine has become available.

Lyme Disease
This is caused by a spirocheate (spiral-shaped) bacterium. It is a tick-borne disease causing acute, often recurrent, polyarthritis in both dogs and humans. The causal agent is *Borrelia burgdorserei*. Fever, cardiac, kidney, and neurological problems can also occur in some cases. A vaccine is available in North America.

PARASITE CONTROL
Parasite control is important for all dogs, whether kept for working duties or for pleasure.

Ectoparasites
Fleas are the most common ectoparasites found on dogs. They are found worldwide and are certainly no strangers to the Rottweiler with his dense, although shortish, double coat.

Some Rottweilers will often carry a very high flea burden, apparently without problems, whereas others will show signs of flea allergy dermatitis, sometimes as the result of a very light flea infestation. This is due to the development of a hypersensitivity to flea saliva. This, thankfully, is relatively rare in the Rottweiler compared with some other breeds, but when it occurs, it presents major problems both for dog and owner.

It causes serious itching and these dogs often have large, hairless patches and are continually scratching. Since the itching (pruritis) is due to the allergic reaction and not to the actual irritation of flea bites, and since fleas do not spend their whole time on the dog, owners often find it difficult to believe that the condition is indeed due to fleas since, despite careful examination, they have never seen a flea on the dog.

Fleas are not host-specific. Dog and cat fleas can be found on dogs, cats, and humans. All types of fleas can bite all species of animals, including man.

The dog flea— Ctenocephalides canis.

The Life Cycle of the Flea

Flea control becomes more logical if a little is known about the life cycle of the flea. Eggs and the larval (immature) form of the flea develop off the host. Development time depends upon both humidity and temperature. In warm environments, particularly with high humidity, the life cycle is completed in days. This is one of the reasons why fleas are such a problem in Britain in warm summers and in the southern United States all year round. The widespread use of central heating has also added to the problem.

Fleas can survive in suitable environments for more than a year without feeding. This is the reason why dogs and people can get bitten when entering properties left unoccupied, often for long periods of time, after having harbored pets.

Effective flea control involves dealing with adult fleas on the dog and the immature stages that develop off the dog in the environment. Obviously control of developing fleas in the yard is not practicable, particularly if continuously reinfested from visiting wildlife. These can vary from bats to raccoons, depending on the situation.

Fleas have to have a meal of blood to complete their life cycle. They feed on the dog, then lay eggs that develop in the environment. These may actually be laid on the dog and drop off, or the fleas may hop off the dog in order to lay them.

In the home, control should include thorough vacuuming to remove all the immature stages. The use of an environmental insecticide with prolonged action to kill any developing fleas must be considered, since few insecticides currently on the market will kill flea larvae.

Flea Control

Control of fleas on the dog can involve oral medication taken by the dog to prevent completion of the life cycle of the flea. The flea

A spray can be used to eradicate fleas.

Spot-on preparations give protection for up to two months.

ingests the compound when it bites the dog for a blood meal. In addition, sprays, powders, and spot-on preparations can be used to kill any adult fleas present. Insecticidal baths effectively kill adult fleas on the dog but do not usually have any lasting effect; therefore, bathing must always be combined with other methods of flea control.

Some Rottweilers are upset by the noise of sprays, while powders tend to be messy and to be shed on carpets and soft furnishings. Therefore, modern spot-on preparations, which will give reasonable protection lasting up to two months, are probably the most effective. These work even if your dog is bathed between applications. They disperse a chemical throughout the invisible fat layer that covers the skin of a healthy dog. The chemical is thus not absorbed into the body. Within 24 hours of application, the dog will have total protection against fleas since, on biting, the flea's mouthparts have to penetrate through the fat layer to get to the blood and, in this way, the flea absorbs the parasiticide.

Oral medication preventing completion of the life cycle of the flea is effective for long-term control but will not be of immediate help to the allergic dog. Scratching is caused by the dog's reaction to the saliva from the bite of the adult flea seeking the essential blood meal in order to reproduce.

Lice

Lice are not as common as fleas. Unlike fleas, the whole life cycle occurs on the host and the eggs (nits) are sticky and attach to individual hairs. Lice cause intense pruritis (itching) and are not uncommon on Rottweiler puppies that are the products of puppy farms (puppy mills) and, sometimes, on adult dogs that live in rural locations. Eradication is relatively simple since most flea preparations are effective, as is bathing with insecticidal shampoo.

Ticks

Ticks can be a problem in some areas, on both sides of the Atlantic. They are important since they can be the carriers of various diseases that can affect your Rottweiler. Lyme disease, babesiosis, and ehrlichiosis are examples.

Many of the flea and louse preparations are also licensed for tick control. Some of the spot-on preparations, in particular, have prolonged activity even if the dog is bathed several times between applications.

Harvest Mites

These are the immature forms (larvae) of a mite that lives in decaying organic matter. The tiny

Ticks are likely to affect dogs that live in rural areas.

red larvae are just visible to the naked eye and are picked up by dogs exercised in fields and woodland locations particularly with chalky soils. The feet and muzzle are most commonly affected.

The use of prolonged-action insecticidal preparations is recommended since reinfestation is likely, particularly if your Rottweiler is exercised in the locations described earlier.

Cheyletiellosis—"Walking Dandruff"

Walking dandruff is an apt description! The causal mite, *Cheyletiella yasguri*, can just be seen by the naked eye. Cheyletiella infection is not uncommon in farm-reared Rottweilers. Puppies will appear to be itchy, especially along the mid-line of the back. On close examination, this area appears to have a lot of dandruff, some of which appears to move—the mites themselves! Treatment with any of the usual insecticidal preparations, baths, sprays, etc., is effective.

Although it is usually puppies that are affected and the mite lives only on the host, adult dogs can act as symptomless carriers. The mite is zoonotic, i.e., it will affect humans, particularly children, and causes intense irritation.

Mange

Rottweilers are not particularly prone to mange but it can occur, particular in puppy farm- (puppy mill-) produced stock. Mange is a parasitic skin disease caused by microscopic mites. Two types of mange can cause problems in dogs.

Demodectic mange

The demodectic mite lives in the hair follicles and causes a problem only in animals whose immune system is incompetent for any reason.

Sarcoptic mange—scabies

Sarcoptic mange is seen more commonly in the Rottweiler. The causal mite lives not in the hair follicles, but burrows in the surface layers of the skin. This form of mange is extremely contagious and also extremely itchy.

The mites are fairly host-specific but dogs can become infected from foxes, raccoons, rabbits, coyotes, and, of course, other dogs. It is transmissible to humans, particularly children, and causes scabies. If mange is suspected, consult your veterinarian without delay. Treatment is dependent upon accurate diagnosis of the causal organism.

Endoparasites

These include, particularly, roundworms and tapeworms. Hookworms, together with heartworm, which is important in Southern Europe and North America, need to be controlled regularly. Worms are the most important endoparasite in Rottweilers, although there are others that can cause problems, e.g., coccidia and giardia, which are macroscopic, one-celled organisms that occasionally cause diarrhea and lack of growth, particularly in poorly reared puppies.

Roundworms

These are the most common worms in the dog. *Toxocara canis,* the most common roundworm, is a large, round, white worm 3–6 inches (7–15 cm) long. The worm undergoes a complicated life cycle in the dog and larvae (immature forms) can remain dormant in the tissue of adult dogs for long periods. In the female, under the influence of the hormones of pregnancy, these immature forms become activated. They cross the placenta and finally develop into adult worms in the small intestines of the puppy. There is a slight risk that humans, particularly children, can become infected, and therefore regular worming of your Rottweiler (at least twice a year) is a wise precaution.

Rottweiler puppies with heavy worm infestations can show signs ranging from generalized poor growth to diarrhea and vomiting, obstruction of the bowel, and even death in cases of extreme worm burdens.

Reinfection occurs from infected larvae developing from eggs passed in feces. Regular worming is, therefore, recommended. Consult your veterinarian.

Regular worming will prevent repeated roundworm infestation.

Tapeworms

Tapeworms, or cestodes, are the other major class of worms found in the dog. They differ from roundworms in that they have an indirect life cycle. This means that spread is not directly from dog to dog, as in the case of roundworms, but must involve an intermediate host. These vary according to the type of tapeworm.

Dipylidium caninum, the most common tapeworm in the dog (and cat), uses the flea as the intermediate host. These worms can measure up to 20 inches (50 cm) and live in the intestine. Many eggs are contained within mature segments that look like grains of rice and are shed from the end of the worm and passed in the dog's feces.

The eggs are microscopic. Immature stages of the flea, which are free living (flea larvae), ingest the microscopic eggs that mature as the flea develops. The mature flea is then swallowed by the dog and so the life cycle of the tapeworm is completed. Effective tapeworm remedies are on sale in pet supply stores and supermarkets without prescription, but since effective control also involves rigorous flea control, it is worthwhile discussing the problem with your veterinarian.

Another type of tapeworm of importance is *Echinococcus granulosus*. This is found on both sides of the Atlantic, although it is relatively rare in the U.K. It is a small tapeworm, only about one-quarter of an inch (6 mm) long. It lives in the intestine of the dog but the intermediate host is the sheep, so Rottweilers kept as herding dogs can be at risk. It is important because it can also affect man (zoonotic).

If your Rottweiler is fed raw meat unfit for human consumption (dog meat), it may be infected with the *Taenia* species of tapeworm. This also occurs if the dog is allowed to catch and eat prey, since intermediate hosts include rabbits, hares, and similar wildlife.

Most tapeworm infections occur in adult dogs. Usually the first signs noted by most owners are little wriggling "rice grains" around the dog's anus. These are the mature segments containing eggs that have to be eaten by the intermediate host to complete the life cycle.

Effective tapeworm remedies cover all types of tapeworm and should be administered regularly, usually about twice a year. Consult a veterinarian.

Heartworm—*Diarofilaria immitis*
This is a major problem in many warmer parts of the world. It does occur in Great Britain but,

to date, only in imported animals. Transmission is by bites from mosquitoes. Very effective remedies are available.

Hookworms, Whipworms, and Lungworms
These can also cause problems in certain areas. Your veterinarian will advise if any special remedies or precautions have to be taken.

EXERCISE
Exercise is a most important area of preventive care. Hip dysplasia and other bone problems, e.g., osteochondrosis dessicans (OCD)—to be dealt with later—do occur in the breed. Therefore, exercise must be controlled, particularly while your Rottweiler is immature.

Once fully mature, a Rottweiler needs regular exercise to keep him mentally and physically occupied.

That means restricted exercise until approximately 12–18 months of age (see Chapter Two).

Your three-month-old Rottweiler will find a quarter of an hour's basic leash training just as exhausting as an hour's walk. At three months old, an hour's walk is not the best thing for those rapidly developing and, possibly, hip dysplasia-prone joints. A quarter of an hour in the yard on a leash and your puppy will sleep for hours.

Broadly, the more active the puppy, the more sleep and rest is needed, so half an hour of training and four hours of sleep at six months of age makes a good combination. You can then profit by the skills learned at the training class: a quarter of an hour leash-walking and contentment will reign!

Once over a year old, exercise must be adequate for the dog's needs; otherwise, boredom will supervene. These are not dogs for sedentary owners.

The inability to stimulate, extend, and exercise the young, healthy adult Rottweiler can lead to major behavioral problems, which are clearly not the dog's fault. This has to be accepted as one of the responsibilities of owning this dominant breed.

EMERGENCY CARE AND FIRST AID

Accidents and emergencies occur with any dog and the Rottweiler, no matter how well trained, is no exception. Emergencies involve not just road traffic and other accidents; bites, burns, heatstroke, insect stings, and poisonings can all occur unexpectedly.

Because of their size, their active extrovert nature, and the ever-present danger of broken glass in urban and suburban situations, Rottweilers are particularly prone to cuts involving their feet and pads, and these are sometimes very severe. Therefore, an emergency kit, with a good supply of large bandages, is a wise precaution in a Rottweiler household.

First aid is the initial treatment given to an emergency. The purpose is to preserve life, reduce pain and discomfort, and minimize the risk of permanent disability and disfigurement. No matter what the emergency, there is much that can be treated by simple first aid.

Priorities
- Keep calm and do not panic.
- Get help. Contact your veterinarian, explain the situation, and obtain first aid advice.
- If there is a chance of internal injury, try to keep your dog as still as possible, placing him on his side on the ground. The head and neck can be gently pressed to the ground with your arm across the neck, if necessary holding uninjured limbs and partially lying across him. However, try not to place your weight on his chest since this could interfere with breathing.
- If he is in shock, try to keep him as warm as possible. Use blankets if available or wrap him in a coat or even newspaper.
- Moving any injured large-breed dog is always difficult. The Rottweiler is no exception. If only one limb is injured, most dogs can be encouraged to move, with a little patience and support from people they know. However, do take care. Your dog may

The responsible owner should learn the principles of first aid.

be in pain and frightened, and may bite unexpectedly and totally uncharacteristically.

- If the dog cannot move, try rolling him onto a blanket. Then, if there are sufficient helpers, each taking a corner, he can be carried and lifted into a vehicle.
- If at all possible, get someone to travel in the back of the car with the dog when you take him to the veterinarian.
- Drive carefully and observe the speed limits.

Shock

Shock is a complex condition, disrupting the delicate fluid balance in the body. It always results in a serious drop in blood pressure. This can be due to severe bleeding, heart failure, acute allergy, heatstroke, etc.

First signs include rapid breathing and increased heart rate. The mucous membranes, e.g., of the gums, lips, or under the eyelids,

look pale, and the dog may appear depressed. His feet or ears may feel cold to the touch. Vomiting may occur.

- Try to keep the dog as warm as possible. Cover him with coats, blankets, or even newspapers.
- Keep as quiet as possible. Seek immediate veterinary help, particularly if hemorrhaging is present. If at all possible, try to control bleeding using finger or hand pressure if nothing else is available.

The ABCs of First Aid

Attention should always be directed first to

- A—AIRWAY (Make sure there is no obstruction preventing oxygen reaching the lungs.)
- B—BREATHING (Check that this is occurring.)
- C—CARDIAC FUNCTION (Is the heart beating?)

Airways

It is vital to maintain these three essential functions, but do not take risks. For example, it is not uncommon for a young Rottweiler to get a ball or other object stuck in the throat when playing. Be very careful about putting your fingers in the mouth: the dog will be fighting for his breath and, even though normally placid, may bite in fright. Try to open his mouth using a suitably padded stick, or even a tie or pair of panty hose to pry the jaws apart. Sometimes, a ball stuck in the back of the throat can be dislodged by pressure on the throat from the outside, and behind, forcing the obstruction forward through the mouth.

Breathing

If he is not breathing, try gently pumping the chest with your hand, at the same time feeling behind the elbow to see if you can find a heartbeat (pulse). If not, convert your chest compression to cardiac massage by placing both hands round the chest, just behind the elbows, over the heart. Squeeze approximately 15–20 times a minute. This will have the dual function of stimulating the heart and, at the same time, the compression and relaxation will help to fill the lungs. Stop every 10 squeezes or so to see if you can detect a heartbeat or any breathing.

Bleeding

Cut pads have already been mentioned. These, like torn nails (which are not uncommon in active, exuberant Rotties), are extremely painful and can bleed profusely.

Try to bandage the injury tightly, using any clean material if bandage is not readily available. A plastic bag placed over the paw, between the layers of bandage, will contain the blood. The aim is to apply as much bandaging as possible and then get your dog to the veterinarian without delay, thus ensuring that blood loss has been kept to a minimum.

Do not leave a tight bandage in place for more than 15–20 minutes. If necessary, partially unwrap the bandage and then reapply. If the site cannot be bandaged, try to control the bleeding by applying finger or hand pressure, if possible,

with a piece of clean dressing between your hand and the wound.

Burns and Scalds

These can happen very unexpectedly. Cool the burned area with cold water as quickly as possible. Use wet towels if extensive. Caustics (e.g., drain and oven cleaners, etc.) can burn. Try to dilute with plenty of cold water. If in the mouth, wash it out using cloths soaked in clean, cold water pressed between the jaws.

Eye Injuries

These are not uncommon in the breed, due to foreign bodies, grass seeds, or scratches from cats' claws, bushes, etc. Cover the eye with a pad soaked in cold water or, better still, a saline solution (such as contact lens solution) and then seek veterinary help as soon as possible.

Heatstroke

Rottweilers are not particularly prone to heatstroke. It can occur as a result of being left in cars with too little ventilation in hot weather. Remember, the car need not necessarily be in direct sunlight to kill your dog.

First signs are excessive panting with obvious distress; unconsciousness and coma quickly follow. Try to reduce body temperature by bathing the dog in copious amounts of cold water, iced if possible, and then cover the still-wet animal in damp towels. Take him to the veterinarian as soon as possible. If driving there, make sure that there is plenty of air over the dog—keep the windows open

Never leave your Rottweiler unattended in a parked car.

during the trip. Evaporation will help to reduce his temperature.

Seizures

Convulsions or seizures can occur for a variety of causes, but Rottweilers are, fortunately, not particularly prone to these conditions. However, any dog in a seizure is always a frightening experience for the onlooker. It is better not to touch the dog while he is in the seizure so that he is not stimulated further. Left alone, injury is unlikely, particularly if any moveable furniture (stools, occasional tables, etc.) are moved out of the way.

A dark environment speeds recovery, so keep the light level low, draw the curtains, and turn off any lights. Once recovered, the dog will be dazed and unable to see or hear properly for a short time, so use caution in handling him because he may be frightened and may not recognize you.

As soon as possible, take him to your veterinarian.

BREED-SPECIFIC PROBLEMS

Rottweilers are basically very healthy. However, with increasing popularity, certain breed-specific problems have become evident, particularly affecting bones and eyes.

Skeletal Problems

Bone Tumors

As with many large breeds, primary bone tumors (which comprise 3–5 percent of all tumors found in dogs) are not uncommon in Rottweilers. These can be of various types but osteosarcoma, which is a malignant bone tumor, comprises more than 85 percent of all bone tumors, followed by fibrosarcoma (which affects mainly the joints) comprising approximately 10 percent. An early sign is, usually, increasing lameness, often without any other signs such as pain or swelling.

Today, treatments are available that are palliative if not curative, but it is important that treatment is commenced early in the course of the disease. Therefore, if you have any concerns, do not delay in consulting your veterinarian.

Cruciate Ligament Rupture

The stifle, or knee joint, is a very important joint in the dog, just as it is with us. Its stability is maintained by a number of ligaments, two of which occur inside the joint. These, the cruciate ligaments, cross over inside the joint and connect the thighbone (femur) to the shinbone (tibia). They ensure that the joint works as a hinge without any looseness.

Fortunately, the Rottweiler is a healthy breed and suffers from few inherited or breed-specific problems.

Rottweilers are heavy, medium-to-large dogs, with an athletic nature. Therefore, they often damage one of the cruciate ligaments, more commonly the cranial or anterior ligament. This usually results in acute lameness, often when at play. The dog is unable to put the affected hind leg to the ground. There is often rapid swelling and pain. It does appear there may be some inherent weakness in the ligament, since the condition will often affect relatively young, athletic dogs.

Very successful surgical repair is widely available today, but some cases may have to be referred to a veterinary orthopedist.

Again, it is important that treatment is undertaken early in order to minimize permanent damage and arthritis in the joint.

Hip Dysplasia

Dysplasia means abnormal growth or development. Hip dysplasia is a developmental condition that results in abnormal looseness of the hip joints. Many factors contribute to the disease, including heredity, nutrition, trauma, and exercise, and the Rottweiler, in common with many other breeds, is frequently affected with this condition. The genetic component results from the interaction of many genes and, therefore, it is called a polygenic condition; some families appear to be more affected than others.

On both sides of the Atlantic, there are screening schemes in place in an attempt to reduce the amount of hip dysplasia within the breed. In the U.K., this health plan is run jointly by the British Veterinary Association and the Kennel Club. The dog is x-rayed in a standard position by your veterinarian. X rays are then scored by a panel of specially trained veterinary experts selected by the British Veterinary Association. A maximum score of 53 is awarded to each hip so that the worst possible hips would score 106. Under this plan, breed mean scores (BMS) are published with the advice that breeders wishing to reduce the risk of hip dysplasia should choose stock with scores well below the BMS.

The number of Rottweilers scored under the plan as of October 6, 1999, was nearly 8,000 with a range from 0–99 with a BMS of 13.

If you are contemplating buying a Rottweiler, it is advisable to ask if the parents have been scored for hip dysplasia and to ascertain the individual score. The puppy will not have been scored since, under the scheme, puppies are not eligible until they are over 12 months of age.

In the United States, a similar scheme is run by the Orthopedic Federation of America (OFA), which scores dogs at an earlier age under a different system, but the aim is the same, to reduce, if not eradicate, this disabling condition in the breed.

Osteochondritis Dessicans, OCD

This is a condition that results in fissures occurring in growing cartilage in the joints. On occasion, this can result in a loose flap of

The rapid-growing Rottweiler can be prone to OCD.

cartilage in the joint, particularly in the shoulder and the elbow. This occurs between 4–10 months of age when the dog may show sudden signs of acute pain and lameness. Although there is a familial predisposition in certain strains, like hip dysplasia it is multifactorial.

Rottweilers grow particularly rapidly at around four months of age and, if they are allowed to be overactive and bounce around on their joints, problems can occur. Prevention is better than cure; therefore, try to restrict exercise until about one year of age if at all possible since, although the acute signs can be treated, arthritis is likely to follow in spite of treatment and this is irreversible.

Elbow Dysplasia

Other diseases apart from OCD affect the elbow, which can cause lameness in the rapidly maturing animal. Elbow dysplasia has several causes, one of which can be OCD. The condition has recently become the subject of a canine health plan in the U.K. and, like HD, this involves X ray interpretation by a panel of experts.

Eye Problems
Entropion

This involves inversion, or inward rolling of the eyelid margins. It is a condition to which growing Rottweilers seem particularly prone. Primary entropion, i.e., that which is not due to some other basic cause, is seen in some strains of Rottweilers and is probably inherited. The first signs seen in the puppy are usually a wetness

The well-cared-for Rottie that is correctly reared and trained will become a companion that is second to none.

around the eye, with tear overflow. There is usually constant rubbing at the eye. If you see these signs, take your dog to the veterinarian as soon as possible. Surgery may be necessary but there are several techniques available and prognosis is usually extremely good. One or both eyes may be affected. Your veterinarian may refer you to an ophthalmologist.

Retinal Dysplasia

The term dysplasia means abnormal growth. Multifocal retinal dysplasia (MRD) in the Rottweiler involves disruption of part of the light-sensitive surface—the retina—in the eye. Often the condition has little or no effect on vision and is only picked up during a routine eye examination by your veterinarian.

In addition to genetics, there are other causes, including drugs and infection, that can result in these nonpainful abnormalities in the developing retina. It is wise to take advice from your veterinarian before breeding your Rottweiler if it is confirmed that the condition is present.

Unlike the other breed-specific problems discussed, MRD is nonpainful and only in extreme cases causes vision impairment.

SUMMARY

From a health care point of view, the Rottweiler is a good dog to own. The breed is not beset with major problems, but it is a rapidly growing breed and preventive health care should encompass training and controlled exercise in addition to nutritional needs and preventive medicine. Early attention to these details results in a healthy, active, and, above all, extremely loyal and obedient companion.

Alexandria-Monroe Public Library
117 E. Church St.
Alexandria, IN 46001